# STAGECOACHES
# & CARRIAGES

*An Illustrated History of*
*Coaches and Coaching*

*Ludgate Circus by Gustave Dore (1850)*

IVAN SPARKES

# STAGECOACHES & CARRIAGES

## An Illustrated History of Coaches and Coaching

Spurbooks Limited

TRANSATLANTIC ARTS, INC.

Levittown, New York 11756

SOLE DISTRIBUTOR FOR THE U.S.A.

Published by


Spurbooks Ltd
6 Parade Court
Bourne End
Buckinghamshire



© Ivan Sparkes 1975

SF
305
56

ISBN 0 902875 56 6




Made and printed in Great Britain by
The Garden City Press Limited
Letchworth, Hertfordshire SG6 1JS

# CONTENTS

# ILLUSTRATIONS

# INTRODUCTION

Throughout the ages, man has cursed, abused, yet revelled in new forms of transport, and has happily leap-frogged from one to another, leaving only the historian, the poet and the philosopher to recall with regret the quieter times left behind. Fortunately for us, the diaries of the last three hundred years abound with comments of everyday travel, of terrible accidents, and of amusing incidents, while the prose of Dickens and Fielding, to name but two, bring to life the busy life of the road.

Perhaps the annoyance of Arthur Young over the bad conditions of the roads in the 18th century, and the absolute pleasure of Pepys in his new coach in the 17th century are but a few reasons for writing a book on coaches and coaching. Nowadays, with the highways pushing their way further into the countryside, we can at least echo the words of John Gay:

> O happy street, to rumbling wheels unknown,
> No carts, no coaches shake the floating town.
> Thus was of old, Britannia's city bless'd,
> Ere pride and luxury he soon profess'd.

While it may be presumptuous to thank Samuel Pepys, Celia Fiennes and other diarists for their help in writing this history, much gratitude must go to the many writers whose works are listed in the bibliography, to those museums who sent brochures, and to the other organisations who helped in locating the illustrations. I must also thank my father, whose recollections of the last days of the Bath Coach driving into Swindon with the post-horn note echoing in the air, spurred me on the way to completion.

IVAN SPARKES
High Wycombe. 1975

# 1

## EARLY TRAVEL AND THE PRIVATE COACHES

'Coaches and sedans, they deserve both to be throwne into the Thames, and but for stopping the channell, I would they were.' This was the opinion of the Watermen in the early 17th century as they saw their passengers being taken from them by the new-fangled vehicles. Their comments were echoed by John Taylor, the water poet, (1580–1653), who wrote a pamphlet in 1623 entitled prophetically 'The World runnes on Wheeles'. This had some very unkind things to say about road transport in general. He recalls that 'the mischiefs that have been done by them are not to be numbered; as breaking of legs and arms, overthrowing down hills, over bridges, running over children, lame and old people, as Henry the fourth of France, he and his Queen were once like to have been drowned, the coach overthrowing besides a bridge; and so to prove that a coach owed him an unfortunate trick; he was some few years after his first escape, most inhumanely and traitorously murdered in one, by Raniliacke, in the streets at Paris.'

The reaction shown by the Watermen and by John Taylor was also that of the ordinary public, for when one of the first coaches came on the road, John Stowe, the historian, (1525–1605), reported, 'In the year 1564 one William Boonen, a Dutchman brought first the use of coaches hither, and the said Boonen was Queen Elizabeth's coachman, for indeed a coach was a strange monster in those days, and the sight of them put both horse and man into amazement; some said it was a great crab-shell brought out of China, and some imagined it to be one of the Pagan Temples in which the cannibals adored the Devil'. He continues, 'After a while divers great ladies; with a great jealousie of the Queen's displeasure; made their coaches and rid them up and down the country to the great admiration of all the beholders'.

*The Assassination of Henry IV of France while travelling in a coach, 1610*

*Early carriage from an illustration in the Luttrel Psalter, c.1338. (Science Museum)*

In spite of the impression these comments give, the use of coaches, or carriages was not new, and their appearance in one form or another, goes back several centuries before the time about which Taylor and Stowe were writing. A description of the Wat Tyler Rebellion of 1381 notes that 'coaches were not known in this island; but chariots or whirlicotes then so called, and they only used of princes or men of high estate'. Thus the reaction to men of lesser class using them, was swift and predictable.

In 1294 Philip the Fair of France issued an ordinance or edict suppressing luxury and forbidding citizen's wives from using carriages. At this time they were used chiefly by women, and when Count Wolf of Barby was called to attend a convention of the States by John Frederick, Elector of Saxony, he had to request special leave on account of ill health to travel to Spires in a coach.

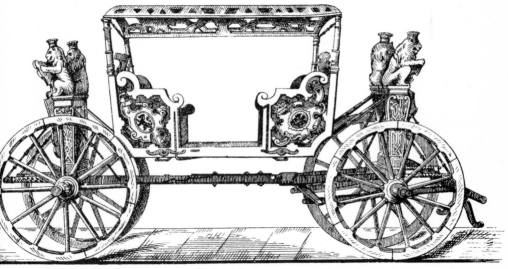

*Wedding coach of Duke of Saxony. (Science Museum)*

Perhaps France and England were behind other countries in introducing these new conveyances. In 1560, at a time when there were only three coaches in Paris, one of which belonged to the King's mistress, and just two in England, over five hundred coaches rode the streets of Antwerp. Of course the label of effeminacy often restricted their use. This was the case in 1558 when Julius, Duke of Brunswick, issued a prohibition against their use. He looked back with fondness on the glorious days of Germany, when its heroes were 'so much celebrated among all nations on account of their manly virtues', but now he noted, 'with great pain and uneasiness that their useful discipline and skill in riding in our electorate country and Lordship have not only visibly declined, but have' been almost lost . . . and as the principal cause of this is that our vassals, servants, and kinsmen without distinction, young and old have dared to give themselves up to indolence and to riding in coaches', their use was forbidden.

In England in the mid-16th century, few coaches were evident, although one contemporary writer refers to Queen Mary's use of one 'The xxx day of September (1553) the Queen's Grace came from the Tower through London riding in a charret gorgeously beseen, unto Westminster'. This chariot was apparently covered with a 'cloth of tissue' and drawn by six horses. Most probably other owners in England were among the more travelled lords, nobles and statesmen. Sir Thomas Hoby of Bisham Abbey, one time Ambassador to France is believed to have owned a coach in 1556, as he offered to lend it to Lady Cecil, his sister-in-law.

Only a few years later we also find in the account books of the Kytson Family of Hengrove, regarding payments for the year 1573:

> For my mistress' coche, with all the furniture theretoe belonging except horses . . . xxxiiij li xiiijs (£34.70)
> For the painting my Mr and Mrss armes upon the coche ijs vjd (2.6d)

Despite such references, available for many years, some sources still quote the year 1580 as the date when the coach was introduced into this country. This may be due to the fact that the 16th-century coach differed from other earlier carriages by being covered or enclosed, and also the body was suspended, being swung above the wheels. It was this kind of coach which was imported from Germany by the Earl of Arundel in 1579 and later, in 1598, specific mention of such a method of suspension was made in bills for six shillings for two new bearing braces for the 'double hanging' of the coach, mentioned in the notebooks of Thomas Screven *c.* 1596. This was an elaborate vehicle, which for the upholstery used 'four skynnes of orange colour leather goate, a covering in black leather; curtaynes, and setting on the firinge'. The inside was brightened with a seat and bed made from nine yards of 'marygold coulour velvet'.

The coach of Queen Elizabeth I, which John Taylor had likened to a giant crab, was of wood carved in a shell pattern. 'The whole composition contains many beautiful curves. The Shellwork creeps up to the roof, which it supports, and which is dome-shaped. The roof is capped by five waving ostrich feathers, one at each corner, and the fifth on the centre of roof, springing from a king of crown.' This coach was drawn by two horses, but was apparently far from comfortable, for when in 1568, the French Ambassador was granted an audience, he found the Queen complaining bitterly of aching pains from the bruising suffered the previous day due to the coach being driven too fast. So when Elizabeth I came to Norwich in 1578, writes Sir Thomas Browne. 'She came on horseback . . . but she had a coach or two in her trayne'.

Another type of vehicle had a small boot seat in the rear which was as uncomfortable, for when Edward Barker wrote to his father in 1663, he commented, 'my journey was noe ways pleasant, being forced to ride in the boote all the waye. This travel hath soe indisposed mee, yt I am resolved never to ride againe in yr coach. I am extreamly hot and feverish . . .'

Despite much opposition and criticism, the use of the coach gained favour among the nobility and within twenty years a great trade in coach-making had developed.

Even if the coach-makers met the demands of the gentry, the conditions of the roads did not allow for easy passage. At Bristol the extreme narrowness of the streets would not permit the use of coaches. In London, the roads were so bad that in May 1685, Sir Ralph Verney wrote that when he brought his coach to the capital 'the stones being ready to shake it to pieces'. The absence of sewage and cleansing services also meant that refuse was thrown out of windows, accumulated in the street channels and so caused great nuisance. Damage could also be received from pit falls after dark caused by newly dug vaults, and open flapped cellars where the poorest of the city dwellers lived.

Such was the condition of the roads, that, linked with the increasing interest in coaching, a bill was drafted in 1601 'to restrain the excessive use of coaches in this realme'. As this was not carried, the Attorney General was directed to frame some fit bill touching the use of coaches. Some years elapsed before the proclamation was issued in 1618 which limited coaches to a draught of five horses, on pain of Star Chamber proceedings. Four years later wagons were also included in the prohibition. The proclamation blamed the decay of the highways and bridges on the new use by carriers of four-wheeled wagons, drawn by eight, nine and ten horses, carrying up to sixty or seventy hundredweight.

In a pamphlet of 1673 the writer sees no end to the miseries of travel. 'Is it for a man's health to travel with tired jades, to be laid fast in the foul ways and forced to wade up to the knees in mire, and afterwards to sit in the cold till teams of horses can be sent to pull the coach out! Is it for their health to travel in rotten coaches, and to have their tackle, or perch, or axle-tree broken, and then to wait three or four hours, sometimes half a day to have them mended, and then to travel all night to make good their stage!'

Besides legislating against heavy traffic, under regulations of 1627,

*Hooded travelling car or wagon of the late 16th century. (Science Museum)*

carriers and drovers were forbidden to travel on Sundays, on pain of a fine of twenty shillings, for it was felt that 'The Lord's Day, commonly called Sunday, was much broken and profaned by carriers wagoners, carters, wainsmen, butchers and drovers of cattle, to the dishonour of God and reproach of religion'.

These early coaches showed some experiments in the use of different materials, and the first glass coach was brought into England, according to John Aubrey (1626–97), by the Duke of York shortly after the Restoration. George, Duke of Buckingham (1628–87), soon financed a glass-works at Vauxhall, and in June 1663 he applied for a renewal of his patent for making crystal looking glass and coach glasses. The King's favourite managed to create a monopoly, as in July the following year a proclamation forbad the importing of several types of glass, including window glass.

The introduction of windows caused mishaps, and at one time Lady Peterborough was happily driving along the road when she saw a friend to whom she wished to wave. Without remembering that she was in her new glass coach, she put her head straight through the glass window! Samuel Pepys was also most vexed when he was forced to pay forty shillings for a glass panel for his coach 'which was broke the other day, nobody knows how, within the door, while it was down'.

Meanwhile the English coachmakers were doing well. Just as England had received the new coach from Germany, now, towards the end of the 16th century, John of Finland, on his return to Sweden from England, took a coach which was the first to be seen in Sweden.

As time went by the coach became more accepted and much more necessary to the citizens of the realm. The coaches varied quite considerably in size. Mr Henry Howard, the brother of the Duke of Norfolk had a great coach built for him which could carry up to fourteen people. It was used to carry the lady guests to his New Year parties. This coach was reputed to have cost more than five hundred pounds. The number of coaches in use increased as the noblemen realised how much easier travelling around the countryside became with their use. When Earl Fitzwalter of Moulsham Hall, Chelmsford, visited Harrogate in 1734, he took with him twenty-two relatives, friends and servants. These were moved to the resort with eleven saddle-horses, seven coach-horses, his own carriages and a hired coach and six.

Different types of coaches were developed for different uses. T. A. Croal quotes a few lines of a play by Robert Greene (1560–92):

> Nay for a need, out of his easy native,
> May'st draw him to the keeping of a coach,
> For country and a carroch for London

Travel in the country was much rougher than in London. We find that Squire Western's wife in *Tom Jones* by Henry Fielding (1707–54), had a coach and four usually at her command; though unhappily, indeed, the badness of the neighbourhood and of the roads, made this of little use.

Although the Commonwealth Period (1649–60) did little to foster ostentation or luxury, we find that coaches as a mode of travel were accepted, and that Cromwell himself was often inclined to drive his own coach in Hyde Park for recreation. In a letter from the Dutch Ambassador to the States-General dated 16th October 1654, it is recounted, 'His highness, only accompanied with Secretary Thurloe and some of his gentlemen and servants went to take the air in Hyde Park ... had a mind to drive the coach himself ... but at last provoking the horses too much with the whip they grew unruly and ran so fast that the postillion could not hold them in, whereby His Highness was flung out of the coach upon the pole ... The Secretary's ankle was hurt leaping out, and he keeps to his chamber.'

Not everybody was pleased at Cromwell's safe escape. The cavalier poet John Cleveland (1613–58) could not help rhyming a description of the event which concluded with the lines:

I wish to God, for these three kingdom's sake
His neck, and not the whip, had giv'n the crack.

This accidental falling on the pole or out of the coach happened all too often. During Lady Arabella Stuart's progress of 1609 her accounts show a payment of £2 0s. 0d. to the coachman who had his leg broke. When the coachmen of John Evelyn the diarist, and Henry Howard, were driving their respective masters home from dining with Sir William Ducie, they were so drunk that they both fell from their coach seats on Blackheath.

Evelyn (1620–1706), was travelling abroad just as the new coaches were beginning to appear on the Continent. His diary of the 1640s contains several references to the variety of vehicles he encountered. He was fortunate in 1641 to borrow Sir Henry de Vic's coach and six in Brussels and travel in it to Ghent. In Paris he commented on 'the multitude of coaches passing over the bridge, and the large numbers which filled the Tuileries.' He also saw in Paris some years afterwards a new coach which he liked so much that he noted the design and, according to his diary for 29th May 1652, 'went to give orders about a coach to be made against my wife's coming, being my first coach, the pattern whereof I brought out of Paris'.

When he wrote in 1837, William Bridges Adams (1797–1872) complained of the lack of invention on the part of English coach-makers, remarking that the names of almost all the then popular types reflected a continental origin. Among the first to appear on the scene was the *Berlin* which was originally made in 1660. Various attempts had been made to produce a light swift vehicle, and it was Philip de Chiesa, a Piedmontese in the service of the Duke of Prussia who is reputed to have led the way. These new coaches utilised two perches instead of the single pole previously used. The body of the coach was hung on braces, they could carry one or two persons and so could be constructed as a light travelling carriage. These *Berlins* also featured the use of glass windows.

Soon after, about 1670, the French invention of the gig produced a small, light personal vehicle which did not appear as a serious rival to the *Berlin*, but instead seemed to perform an entirely different function. The gig was basically a chair or seat fixed on to a two wheeled chassis which could be drawn by one horse.

Although mention has been made of hanging the coach on leather braces, attempts by Edward Knapp in 1625 to hang them on springs of steel were not successful. Some forty years elapsed before a Colonel Blunt's work was brought to the notice of the Royal Society, and in 1665 Samuel Pepys joined with 'Lord Brouncker, Sir Frederick Murrey, Dean Wilkins and Mr Hooke, going by coach to Colonel Blunt's to dinner . . . no extraordinary dinner, nor any other entertainment good; but afterwards to the tryal of some experiments about making of coaches easy. And several we tried; but one did prove mightly easy, not here for me to describe, but the whole body of the coach lies upon one long spring, and we all, one after another, rid in it, and it is very fine and likely to take.'

Pepys in his social visits, also met up with Sir William Penn who had just purchased a light chariot. Pepys commented that it was 'plain, but pretty and more fashionable in shape than any coaches he hath, and yet do not cost him, harness and all, above £32'. Obviously Samuel had given some thought to the matter of travel, for on 2nd March 1662 he lay 'talking long in bed with my wife about our frugal life for the time to come, proposing to her what I could and would do, if I were worth £2,000, this is, be a knight, and keep my coach, which pleased her'. Some years elapsed before he felt sufficiently well established to afford this luxury, but the time came when 'I have had it much in my thoughts lately that it is not too much for me now, in degree or cost, to keep a coach, but contrarily, that I am almost ashamed to be seen in a hackney'.

Looking around for a while, he chose a vehicle to which he then

LA SORTIE DE LA REYNE A COMPAIGNE DV ROY DE LA
GRANDE BRETAIGNE SON BEAV FILS DV CHATEAV DE
GIDDE HALLE.

*Coaches in the courtyard of Gidea Hall, Romford, 1637. (Romford Library)*

*Coach of the Stuart period covered with leather and studded with nails*

took a strong dislike. A friend, Mr Povey agreed, stating, 'he finds infinite fault with it, both as to being out of fashion and heavy, with so good reason that I am mightily glad of his having corrected me in it'. Eventually a satisfactory coach was purchased. But as with any modern car owner, problems soon arose: 'Up and vexed a little to be forced to pay 40s. for a glass of my coach'. Also, people began to talk about his reaching above his station in life. Despite such criticism, Samuel Pepys continued to use his fine coach, even having it newly painted, until in 1669, 'we went alone through the town with our new liveries of serge, and the horse's manes and tails tied with red ribbons and the standards gilt with varnish and all clean, and green reines, the people did mightily look upon us; and the truth is, I did not see any coach more pretty, though more gay, than ours all the day'.

This reaction of other people to owners of coaches was fairly common, for in John Gilpin's immortal ride we find:

> *The morning came, the chaise was brought*
> *But yet was not allowed*
> *To drive up to the door, lest all*
> *Should say that she was proud.*
>
> *So three doors off the chaise was stopped*
> *When they did all get in*
> *Six precious souls and all agog*
> *To dash through thick and thin.*

The number of coaches continued to increase and fill the streets, until in 1668 over one thousand were estimated to have assembled in Hyde Park to view the muster of the Life Guards in the presence of the King and the Duke of York. Their use as a compliment or token of respect was apparent when over two hundred accompanied Lord Clarendon from London to St Albans in 1685 when he left for Dublin. At funerals, as today, the number of coaches indicated the importance of the deceased.

*The gallows at the Old Bailey, c.1785*

Persons of high rank sentenced to death could avoid that last ride in the open wagon by following the example of Lord William Russell and be brought in their own coach to the scaffold. For the common criminal the wagon was much more practical. According to Horatio Busino, Chaplain to the Venetian Ambassador in London in 1618, "They take them five and twenty at a time . . . on a large cart like a high scaffold. They go along quite jollily, holding their sprigs of rosemary and singing songs, accompanied by their friends and a multitude of people . . . the executioner hastens the business, and beginning at one end, fastens each man's halter to the gibbet. They are so closely packed that they touch each other with the hands tied in front of them, wrist to wrist so as to leave them the option of taking off their hats and saluting bystanders. Finally . . . the whip is applied to the cart horses, and thus the culprits remain dangling in the air precisely like a bunch of fat thrushes. They are hard to die of themselves, and unless their own relation or friends pulled their feet or pelted them with brickbats in the breast as they do, it would fare badly with them'.

# 2

## THE KING'S HIGHWAY

By 1769, road traffic had become quite considerable, and the condition of the highways then, and for some two hundred years previously when coaches and carriages began to use the roads, was quite deplorable.

Many of these highways were a legacy from the Romans, but they were still serviceable despite centuries of neglect. Three of them, Watling Street, Ermine Street and Foss Way were regarded as royal roads. These were, by modern standards, little more than dirt roads, very dusty in summer and virtually impassable quagmires in winter. To such conditions were added the stench of decaying horse manure, and the dung from the cattle being driven slowly to market. If these were the main roads, consider the state of the minor ones. Meandering cart tracks in which fallen trees, broken bridges and flooded streams would stay unnoticed and unrepaired for many months at a time.

On the royal roads the travellers were deemed to have the king's protection, and a fine of one hundred shillings could be imposed on anyone attacking a fellow-traveller. The roads were originally fairly wide, as they had to be of sufficient width to allow two wagons to pass or sixteen armed knights to ride abreast. The Statute of Winchester (1285) 'commended that highways from one merchant town to another shall be broadened wherever there is underwood or hedges or ditches so that there be no ditch, tree nor bush where a man can lurk or do mischief within two hundred feet of either side of the road'. This confirmed the early Great Charter of 1215 in which was incorporated a promise that 'all merchants shall have safe conduct to go and come out of and into England, and to stay in or travel through England by land for purchase or sale ... except in time of war'.

An important aspect of travel on the roads was linked with the pilgrims. From early days the roads of Europe were peopled with rich and poor alike, all seeking absolution by a visit to a holy shrine. Besides the great centres of Rome and Jerusalem, many holy relics at sites in France and Spain attracted the pilgrims. Centres in England were linked by a network of minor roads and guest houses and monasteries along the route gave shelter and comfort to the weary travellers. The monasteries too had been active in maintaining the roads and bridges in their vicinity, for they owned large tracts of land, and many bridges were repaired and some road work carried out regularly to aid the traveller.

*The Cambridge Telegraph Stagecoach*

When the monasteries were dissolved by Henry VIII in the 1530s, their duties were often left unattended, and just as the loss of their guest houses and hospitals was a blow to the travelling community, so, when the vast buildings and lands of the religious orders were sold, the new owners did not necessarily follow their example in keeping the roads in a reasonable state.

Some attempts to introduce legislation were made, such as the Act of 1523 which allowed a land owner in Kent to enclose an old road and make a new one. Similar Acts were passed, for Sussex and London, the latter between 1534 and 1540, which re-echoed the instructions of Edward III that the roads out of London, in this case between Temple Bar and Westminster, be re-surfaced. It also stipulated that landowners of each side should make good a footpath seven feet wide. The roads at one point were laid down by a Royal Court to be at least eighteen feet wide, a distance which allowed two wagons to pass.

The state of the country roads was further reduced by the continual use of ploughs. A form of plough with a box attachment was used for carrying stones or other goods. At a later date the Bridgewater Sessions (1614 and 1622), prohibited their use on newly made

*Repairing the Strand 1851. (Science Museum)*

roads, imposing penalties of six shillings and eightpence at one point, and five shillings at another. Just as some wealthy left money to charity, others bequeathed sums of money for the repair or upkeep of some particular road or bridge. Henry Clifford, Earl of Cumberland, left one hundred marks to be used on the roads in Craven and another hundred marks for the roads of Westmorland. This was the result of a journey which the Earl undertook and reported as a formidable experience. In 1592 John Lyon bestowed the rents of some properties for repairs on the roads from Harrow and Edgware to London, for, as founder of Harrow School, he was anxious to keep the road open. While in the Midlands, Sir John Stokton, bearing in mind the importance of Wycombe's Cornmarket in the 15th century, left £40 in his will for the repair of the road from Holtspur 'to the end of the town of Great Wycombe and from Wycombe to West Wycombe'. He stipulated that the road should be widened and the overhanging trees cut down.

The legislation which was the start of the new order, came in the reign of Queen Mary with the Highways Act of 1555. This, in its preamble notes that the roads were 'tedious and noisome to travel on, and dangerous to passengers and carriages'. The conclusion of the writers of the Act was that the parish was to be responsible for the roads within its boundaries, and that 'the Constables and Church-wardens of every parish shall yearly, upon the Tuesday or Wednesday in Easter week, call together a number of parishiners, and shall then elect and choose two honest persons of the parish to be surveyors and orderers for one year of the works for amendments of the highways in their parish'.

The job of the surveyors involved keeping accounts of the work done, making a survey of all roads and bridges three times a year, ensuring the roads were kept clear of overhanging trees or encroach-ments from the landowners, and finally ensuring that all parishioners played their part in the repair of the roads. This job was not only unpaid, but the unlucky person could be fined £5 if he would not accept the office when asked. Another drawback lay in the fact that doctors and clergymen were exempt and the gentry were usually not involved, so it was an innkeeper or farmer, usually with a knowledge of road repair, who got the unwanted position.

There was always a problem in ensuring that the villagers did their full amount of road work. The Act of 1555 laid down that every person with land valued at over £50 must send 'one wain or cart furnished after the custom of the county, with oxon, horses or other cattle, and all other necessities meet to carry things convenient for that purpose, and also two able men with the same'. Farmers had to provide a man with a horse, while every householder and labourer had to work on the road, or send someone in his place, for eight hours on four days announced by the surveyors. As this amount of time proved insufficient, it was increased to six days in 1562.

The money for material came chiefly from the fines, which were charged if labourers or teams did not appear. By 1670 these were fixed at one shilling and sixpence a day for a labourer, three shillings for a man with a horse, while the absence of the cart with its two attendant labourers caused a fine of ten shillings a day to be enforced.

Very soon it was apparent that people preferred to pay rather than work. William Harrison, writing in about 1560, commented that 'the rich do so cancel their portions and the poor so loiter in their labours, that of all the six, scarce two good days work are performed'. This unwillingness, which was quite natural, is also echoed in the *Gentleman's Magazine* of December 1767. 'Statute Labour is a burden from which everybody has endeavoured, and always will endeavour, to screen themselves and one another. Teams and labourers coming out for statute work are generally idle, careless and under no commands ... they make holiday of it, lounge about and trifle away their time.'

Another writer, Daniel Defoe (1660–1731) published a well thought out plan to keep the road in constant repair at no charge at all. He adopted Gilbert and Sullivan's well known dictum in the Mikado, 'make the punishment fit the crime' for he suggested that sentenced highwaymen and other gaolbirds should be put to work on the King's highway. Sometimes the sheer volume of work was too great for the villagers, even allowing for each one doing his part.

Isaac Walton (1593–1683) agreed about the way in which certain soils did not help the matter, for in Cotton's continuation of *The Compleat Angler* he quotes the proverb, *There is good land where there is foul way.* A variety of substances were put down to level the road and at Maidstone Quarter Sessions in April 1759, a local butcher in the parish of Cranbrook was accused of laying dung, blood and other filth in a certain part of the King's high road at Milkhouse Street in the said parish. John Copeland quotes a labourer in Nottinghamshire who went so far as to dig several holes in the middle of the road in search of coal, and these were so large that 'the King's subjects during the time aforesaid could not pass, return, ride and labour with their horses, coaches, carts and carriages'.

In some areas stone was hard to come by, and the village of Avebury in Wiltshire, situated as it is in the middle of a giant series of ancient stones, used to light fires beneath these ancient monuments to split them so that the stone could be used for buildings and roads. In the Cornwall village of Sennen, a Quaker was elected Surveyor, against his will, and to pay back the people who voted him into office, he removed two granite crosses, breaking them up for use on the roads.

Despite all these attempts on the part of willing and unwilling road workers, there is no doubt that the roads were deteriorating rapidly during the mid to later 18th century. This was a constant cause of complaint and one noble wrote in 1736 that the road between Kensington and London, 'is grown so infamously bad that we live here in the same solitude as we should do if cast on a rock in the middle of the ocean, and all the Londoners tell us that there is between them and us a great impassable gulf of mud'.

*Crossing the Ford, by Thomas Rowlandson. This gives some idea of the conditions in which the coaches travelled*

In London itself the roads were so bad that when George II went to Parliament through King Street and Union Street, faggots had to be placed in the ruts on the day in order to render the passage of the coach more easy. The mud lay everywhere, and a foreign visitor, M. Misson commented in 1697 that he saw women who were 'forc'd to raise themselves upon pattins or goloshes of iron, to keep themselves out of the dirt and wet'. Arthur Young tells of ruts in the roads four feet deep, filled with mud as a result of a wet summer. He adds 'I actually passed three carts broken down in those eighteen miles of execrable memory.'

Much damage to the surfaces was caused by the sharpness of the wheel rims. Defoe, when describing the industries of the Chilterns, refers to the making of fellies, or fellows, which were wooden rims for cart wheels, used in London where regulations forbad the use of iron rings.

Although another duty of the surveyor was to ensure that roads were not impassable due to overhanging branches, when Celia Fiennes was travelling through England in 1698, so little hedging and ditching was carried out that quite often a footman with an axe had to be sent in front to clear the way. As late as 1723 on parts of the London to Canterbury road, two horsemen could not pass one another, 'or even so much as two wheelbarrows'.

Some surveyors were most difficult to get on with. John Terry of Snave in Kent was accused in 1797 because 'his proceedings (were) unjust and unreasonable . . . in making the road crooked when it might be nearly made straight, unjust in not making it straight in the middle to give each proprietor an equal chance to inclose waste land if it is right that he should doe'.

Following the Great Fire of London, many roads were widened and one Dean of St Paul's commenting on the improved conditions says, 'I paid £15 in a single year for repairs on the pavements of London; and I now glide without noise or fracture on wooden pavements.'

John Evelyn, the diarist (1620–1706), discovered another hazard in June 1652. 'I rode negligently under favour of the shade, till, within three miles of Bromley . . . two cutthroats started out, and striking with long staves at the horse and taking hold of the reins threw me down, took my sword, and hauled me into a deep thicket some quarter of a mile from the highway, where they might securely rob me, as they soon did. What they got of money was not considerable, but they took two rings, the one an emerald with diamonds, the other an onyx and a pair of buckles set with rubies and diamonds . . . and that should teach me never to ride near a hedge.'

A much happier experience fell to the lot of Carl Moritz, a German travelling in England in 1782. 'I was now on the road to Oxford. It is a charming fine broad road; and I met on it carriages without number; which, however, on account of the heat, occasioned a dust that was extremely troublesome and disagreeable. The fine green hedges, which border the roads in England contribute greatly to render them pleasant. This was the case in the road I now travelled; for, when I was tired, I sat down in the shade under one of these hedges and read Milton. But this relief was soon rendered disagreeable to me; for, those who rode, or drove, past me, stared at me with astonishment and made many significant gestures, as if they thought my head disranged.'

One of the greatest problems in travel at this time, was not so much the mud, as the actual flood water which in a rainy season would change the road into a raging torrent. Particularly interesting is the casual way in which Roger Thorseley describes his difficulties on 17th May 1695. '... rode by Puckeridge to Ware, where we baited, and had some showers, which raised the washes upon the road to a height that passengers from London that were upon the road swam, and a poor higgler was drowned, which prevented our travelling for many hours, yet, towards evening adventured with some country people ... though we rode to the saddle skirts for some considerable way, but got safely to Waltham Cross where we lodged.'

Other passengers were not always so lucky; in 1799 'of all the deplorable cases ... the loss of Arthur Robinson Esq. his wife and their female servant ... is the most truly afflicting. The Trent, having been unusually swelled by the late incessant rains, the coach unfortunately overturned as it was passing Tittensor ... the regular driver being ill on the roof, when the coach fell, and his having to trust the reins to another is supposed to have been one of the principal causes of the melancholy event ... The other passengers extricated themselves, and were fortunately sav'd. The body of Mrs Robinson was taken out of the coach, and that of the servant was found soon after; but the remains of Mr Robinson were not discovered till the following evening, having floated down with the torrent.'

Such hazards and the treatment of the roads without special renderings meant that when Sir Henry Parnell completed his *Treatise on Roads* in 1836, he could still say, 'The surface of all the roads, until within a few years was everywhere cut into deep ruts; and even now, since more attention has been paid to road works, though the surface is smoother, the bed of material which forms it is universally so thin, that it is weak and consequently exceedingly imperfect. Drainage is neglected; high hedges and trees are allowed to intercept the action of the sun and wind in drying the roads; and many roads, by constantly carrying away the mud from them for a number of years, have been sunk below the level of the adjoining fields so that they are always wet and damp, and extremely expensive to keep in order'.

On some occasions local authorities went to great lengths to ease congestion on the roads. In High Wycombe in 1767, the Common

Council yielded to the Trustees, the right to pull down part of the grammar school and the south transept of the original cruciform building was sacrificed to eliminate the narrow bottle neck at the entrance to Wycombe. Even this was not a satisfactory answer for when the murderers of a local farmer were hanged on a gibbet twenty-eight feet high for all to see in that part of the town, the crowd was so dense that part of the Grammar School wall was pushed down to make room. It is perhaps typical of the age that at a similar event some four years later, booths and stalls were erected on the Rye (the adjacent common) for the convenience of the public who would be flocking into Wycombe to view the spectacle.

# 3

## STAGE WAGONS AND STAGECOACHES

'Ah Mrs Joyner, nothing grieves me like the putting down my coach!' says Lady Flippant in Wycherley's play *Love in a Wood* (1672). 'For the fine clothes, the fine lodging—let 'em go; for a lodging is as unnecessary a thing to a widow that has a coach, as a hat to a man that has a good peruke. She eats and drinks and sleeps in her coach.' For some, however, the coach was not possible, and when it was put down, they must travel by the next best thing, which was usually the stage wagon, a slow, cumbersome, but far the cheaper method of travel in those days.

These wagons had four large wheels and the body was covered with cloth stretched over a wooden framework. They were originally used for the transit of goods and came into use as early as 1500. One famous wagoner, Thomas Hobson, had a thriving business as a carrier between Cambridge and London in the 16th century. On his father's death in 1568, Thomas inherited the 'cart and eight horses, and all that harness and other things thereunto belonging with the nag'. This nag was the horse which was ridden by the wagoner alongside the wagon as it rumbled along the winding roads. Thomas Hobson was also the owner of stables in Cambridge containing some forty horses 'fit for travelling with boots, bridle and whip, to furnish the gentlemen at once, without going from College to College to borrow'. His constant refusal to allow students to choose their horses, making them instead take the horses in strict rotation led to the adoption of the term *Hobson's Choice*, which is still in popular use.

The slowness of this method of travel was noticeable even in those days of gentle life. Fynes Morison in his itinerary of 1617 comments, 'this kind of journey is so tedious by reason they must take wagons very early and come very late to their innes, that none but women and perhaps people of inferior condition travel in this sort'. Certainly there was little comfort or social separation as passengers and goods were jolted to and fro in a higgledy-piggledy fashion. The wagons carried between twenty and thirty people, and as early as 1637 the *Carriers Cosmology* mentions the names and places of call of over two hundred carriers and wagoners. By the time *Angliae Metropolis* was published in 1681 by Thomas de Laune, the number had increased by half as many again.

The attitude of many people to the wagons is reflected in a letter of Edmund Verney in which he supported the maids in their dislike of travelling from the house in Buckinghamshire to London in the wagons, 'for the very name of a wagon is soe offensive to them'. Yet others found it convenient, and was even used by gentlefolk. We read that Lettice, daughter of Sir William Dugdale, travelled from Coventry to London by wagon, and that Samuel Pepys' mother and sister Paulina also returned to Brampton, their home, in 1661, although we understand that Paulina was 'crying exceedingly' during the journey.

Charles Harper notes that it was common for the passengers to select a chairman or spokesman on setting out, whose job it was to agree with the wagoner where they would halt for meals and sleep, to settle up with the landlords for meals, and keep peace on the journey between the travellers. At the inns their host soon distinguished between the wagon passengers and the more élite coach passengers, or the riding gentry. In *Roderick Random*, Tobias Smollett states that he arrived at an inn where the landlord gave the meal first to three young gentlemen who commented, 'The passengers in the wagon might be d----d; their betters must be served before them; they supposed it would be no hardship on such travellers to dine on bread and cheese for one day.'

Jonathan Swift was able to buy comforts when travelling on a wagon from Farnham to Leicester, for, being under the patronage of Sir William Temple, he was able to pay sixpence extra for a bed and clean sheets for the night. While another traveller, Samuel de Sorbiere, who in error took the wagon from Dover to London, complained that not one of his fellow travellers took the slightest trouble to see what became of him at the inns. 'I might have been a bale of goods,' he declares, 'for all the notice they took of me.'

A somewhat romantic picture of the wagoner is given by Charles Harper. 'He knew something of all kinds of weather and met all kinds

of men in his daily journeys, and thus early became something of a
philosopher. With a sack over his shoulders and peace in his mind,
he could meet the rainy days with joke and song or endure even the
wintry horrors of December and January with equanimity; yet when
spring was come and the grass grew green and the bare ruined boughs
of the trees began to be clothed again with leaves, his horses and
himself were decked with ribbons on May Day ... and not even the
blackbird on the hawthorn spray sang a merrier tune, as he drove his
team along their steady pace! '

*Loading up the stage wagon 1816*

But even their steady pace was interrupted from time to time.
Different proclamations reduced the number of horses to a draught
of either five horses or six oxen, and the weight allowed was reduced to
thirty hundredweight in summer and twenty hundredweight in winter.
In order to reduce the churning of the roads, the width of the wheels
was increased to sixteen inches at the rim, although the Ipswich
Journal of 1761 quotes a figure of nine inches. Even so, the wagons
appear most clumsy and unwieldy.

The common stage wagon was estimated to travel about ten to
fifteen miles a day, and the charge to passengers varied from a

halfpenny a mile, to a shilling a day. A journey between London and
Edinburgh in 1780 took about fourteen days at one shilling a day.
As the distance was three hundred and ninety-six miles, speeds of
twenty-eight miles a day were necessary if the wagon was to arrive
in time. The publicans in Furness had a system whereby when the
conductor of the coach appeared in the distance on the summit of
Wrynose Hill on the journey from Whitehaven and Kendal, the
publicans began brewing their beer in order to have a stock of good
drink ready by the time the travellers reached the village.

*A stage wagon*

In 1776, goods travelled at a rate of 2s. 6d. to 3s. od. a hundredweight. Prices in the 1720s had been around £7.00 a ton, but by
1750 competition had reduced this to between £3.00 and £4.00 a ton.

On most roads the carriers would not change their horses, but
employed the same beasts throughout, however long the journey
might be. However, by 1750 the *Flying Stage Wagon* had come into
being, which progressed much more speedily as it changed horses all
along the route. They could travel well in excess of the wagon speed
of three miles an hour and the *Alton and Farnham Machine* of 1750
could accomplish a journey of forty-seven miles in one day by starting

at six o'clock in the morning and reaching its destination the same night. In 1754 the merchants of Manchester started a flying coach with the advertisement stating, 'incredible as it may appear, this coach will actually (barring accidents) arrive in London in four days and a half after leaving Manchester'.

Of course accidents did happen. In 1779 the Bicester stage wagon, with rollers and eight horses, rumbling and lurching its way through the night, was leaving Wycombe between three and four o'clock in the morning, when it passed too close to the wall of the houses in

*Long distance stage wagon showing wagoner riding on his horse alongside.*
(*Science Museum*)

Frogmoor and crushed to death a baker of Islip, who had unfortunately delayed his return home from Wycombe Market. The Wycombe Coroner's Records also describe how in 1792 the dashing *Birmingham Machine or Fly* when speeding along the High Street on Market day caught the smock of a corn dealer on the splinter bar of the coach and flinging him to the ground, caused his death.

Speed of this nature could not often be achieved in the stage wagon or even the Flying stage wagon, but in the journeys of the stage coach itself, such speeds were possible. The American Quaker, John Woolmer, visited England in 1772 and his 'quietism was shocked by the hurry of the stage coaches' which frequently went upwards of one hundred miles in twenty-four hours. The horses were, he alleged, 'killed by hard driving' and the post boys were frozen to death on the winter nights.

Discomfort is the keynote of contemporary reference to such vehicles, and this is probably why they were not initially a great success. They were also rather restricted in their timetable, running only in summer

*Long distance stage wagon*

months, with the wagons carrying passengers in the winter period. Sir John Colie received a letter from his son's tutor requesting that the lad should travel to London on horseback, as the passage by coach involved 'sitting from five in the morning till almost nine at night, plunging in the cold and dirt and dark, and for two whole days with strange company'.

There were a few who were satisfied. William Chamberlayne, writing in 1673, had nothing but praise for these vehicles, describing them as 'commodious both for men and women to travel from London to the principal towns in the country, that the like hath not been known in the world, and that is by stage coaches, wherein one may be transported to any place sheltered from foul weather and foul ways; free from endangering of one's health and one's body by hard jogging or over violent motion, this not only at a low price (about a shilling for every five miles) but with such velocity and speed in one hour as that the posts in some foreign countries cannot make in one day'.

*The Wagon, 1816, by Thomas Rowlandson*

The early stagecoaches were often discarded private coaches, and many were probably of obsolete design. Some however must have been made specially, as one type of stagecoach had baskets attached to the back for the use of lower-class passengers, and luggage. Sir Walter Scott describes a typical stagecoach in his book *The Antiquary* (1816). 'Constructed principally of a dull black leather, thickly studded, by way of ornament with black broad-headed nails tracing out the panels; frames and green stuff or leather curtains. Upon the doors . . . were displayed in large characters the names of the places whence the coach started, and whither it went.' The vehicles often varied somewhat in shape, the roof of the coach in most cases rose into a swelling curve, which was sometimes surrounded by a high iron guard, which in the

*"Toll gate scene" The sheep, gig, horseman and coach to Oxford make up the typical traffic of the times*

Royal Mails, was formed into a large dome, surmounted in the centre by an immense carved and gilt imperial crown. The wheels of these old carriages were large, massive and ill-formed, and usually of a red colour.

As the number of vehicles increased, so reaction built up against the stagecoach, and in 1673 John Cresset offered a well-written pamphlet arguing in favour of their suppression. By an Act in 1694, stagecoaches were licensed at a yearly charge of eight pounds each, and so the stagecoach was accepted, just as the Hackney Coach had been approved some thirty years before. But even if the coaches were licensed to travel, the public did not always find it easy to get permission to move about themselves. During the Commonwealth period, an Act of 1649–50, ordained that an agreement *to be true and faithful to the Commonwealth* had to be made before such a licence could be given:

> Whereas John Willoughly, beinge desirous to visite his children and kindred, and to live sometyme with them, for which end he hath petitioned for a Licence to Travell ... By virtue of which Act ... wee doe give him libberty to travell to Tolland and Sell-worthy, both in Somersettshire, and to Seaton and Axmouth in Deavon, and to retourne againe within seaven monthes after the date hereof.

Just as sometimes a licence was required for travel, so in some few instances, birth or residence in a certain village or town gave remarkable privileges. This was true of the Liberty of Havering in Essex, once the site of the Royal Palace of Havering. A series of Charter had created exemptions from any payments of 'toll, pontage, murage or passage in any city, borough, town, fair, market or other place whatsoever'. Residents even had the right to demand to be returned for trial to their own village if they were arrested for crimes in other parts of the country, thereby ensuring a more favourable verdict on the crime they may have committed.

Finance acted as a bar to travel for most people, and when Lady Springett, the future mother-in-law of William Penn, rushed from London to Arundel to the bedside of her dying husband, she was charged twelve pounds. Parson Woodeford found it necessary to keep a sharp account of his travelling expenses for future reference.

# YORK Four Days Stage-Coach.

*Begins on* Friday *the* 12th *of* April 1706.

ALL that are defirous to pafs from *London* to *York*, or from *York* to *London*, or any other Place on that Road; Let them Repair to the *Black Swan* in *Holbourn* in *London*, and to the *Black Swan* in *Coney-ftreet* in *York*.

At both which Places, they may be received in a Stage Coach every *Monday*, *Wednefday* and *Friday*, which performs the whole Journey in Four Days, (*if God permits*.) And fets forth at Five in the Morning.

And returns from *York* to *Stamford* in two days, and from *Stamford* by *Huntington* to *London* in two days more. And the like Stages on their return.

Allowing each Paffenger 14ḷ, weight, and all above 3*d.* a Pound.

Performed By  { *Benjamin Kingman,*
              { *Henry Harrifon,*
              { *Walter Baynes,*

Alfo this gives Notice that Newcaftle Stage Coach, fets out from York, every Monday, and Friday, and from Newcaftle every Monday, and Friday.

*Reced in p̄t. 05-00-0 of Mr. Bodington for for Monday the 3 of June 1706*

*The York Stagecoach handbill, 1706. (Science Museum)*

Paid at the coach office at Pickwicks for two inside places and one outside to London £4 0.0. viz inside each £1 11s. 6d., outside 17s. od. Paid for refreshment on the road about 2s. 0. To coachman on the road gave 4s. 0. To guard near London gave 1s. 0. To extra luggage 50 lbs at 1½d pd 6s. 0.

The expenses which fell on the would-be coaching companies were considerable It was impossible to organise suitable stopping places, accommodation, meals and changes of horses without incurring con-

*The basket coach 1780, showing a passenger sitting in the basket*

siderable outlay. There would be the hiring charges for the coach if it was not owned by the proprietor, the wages of the stable boys as well as the coachman, who, in the early 19th century would expect eighteen shillings a week plus his keep. Then there were the additional tolls and the excise duty. This latter charge was based on the Stamp Act of 1804 which fixed the rate for a coach licensed to carry four passengers inside at five shillings for the licence and a duty of twopence per mile, with the larger vehicles carrying up to ten passengers inside at eight shillings for the licence and fourpence per mile.

The highest cost, however, would be for the horses. For the average

*The London coach and Regency styles*

vehicle these animals would often be quite poor specimens, and even blind horses were used, the cost in 1833 being an average of £25 each. However, for the fast coaches, much higher prices were paid. An auction of horses in Brighton in 1826 fetched prices in excess of 70 guineas for horses formerly used in the coach *The Monarch.* While a report in 1817 regarding the loss of two horses, placed a value of 100 guineas upon them. Some of the larger Commercial Coaching Proprietors in the 19th century had very large stables, that of Chaplin & Co. maintaining between 1,300 and 1,500 horses to run a total of sixty-four coaches. At the other end of the scale, a carter in co-operation with an innkeeper would take shares in a coach, and run it from his village to London or a nearby large market town without any intention of ever increasing the size of the operation.

To increase his income, the coachman would not be too scrupulous about the number of passengers either on the roof or inside the coach. The Annual Register of 1770 suggests 'it were greatly to be wished that stage coaches were put under some regulation as to the number of persons and quantity of luggage carried by them. Thirty-four persons were in and around the Hertford coach this day, which broke down by one of the braces giving way. One of the outside passengers was killed on the spot, a woman had both her legs broke, another had one leg broke and very few of the number either within or without but were severally bruised'.

The practice continued, for in 1814 the driver of the Exeter coach was fined £40 for carrying more outside passengers than the law allowed. As there were rewards for reporting such misdemeanours, some informants could be over-zealous. In 1799 one who informed on a coach leaving the *Bull & Mouth Inn* had his statement contradicted by a clergyman and another travelling gentleman, and so ended up in prison himself, convicted of perjury.

The condition of some stagecoaches did not allow for roof passengers. Thomas Croal tells of 'A gentleman sitting in the stagecoach at Berwick complained bitterly that the cushion on which he sat was quite wet. On looking up to the roof he saw a hole through which the rain descended copiously. He called to the Coachman who answered, "Ay mony a ane has complained o' that hole".' Similarly a coach depicted in Dickens' *The Story of the Bagman's Uncle* was so ill-kept that 'The doors had been torn from their hinges and removed; the linings had been stripped off, only a shred hanging here and there

*Mr Pinch getting up on top of the coach in Dickens' novel* Martin Chuzzlewit. (*Victoria & Albert Museum*)

by a rusty nail; the lamps were gone; the poles had long since vanished, the ironwork was rusty; the paint worn away'.

Fortunately for the services, not all were so critical, the Baron d'Haussey in 1833 notes, 'One may travel from one end of England to another without hearing the sound of a whip, or the hallooing of the conductors, which in France falls so disagreeably on the ears of the traveller'. It was possibly this peacefulness which commended itself to Mary Verney who sent her three week old baby to travel by stage-coach from St Albans in Hertfordshire to their Buckinghamshire home.

*The* Comet *stagecoach which ran from London to Bristol*

It was, in fact, common practice for some of the gentry to travel part of the way by coach and then transfer to their own or their host's coach for the remainder of the journey. We find that one constant traveller, Sir William Dugdale frequently used the stagecoach for no more than one or two stages out of London, to St Albans or Woburn, where his horse and manservant would be waiting. From there he would complete his journey in his own time.

Naturally, when a coach was obviously paying dividends, it would have been most frustrating to have a pirate service commence on the same route, and so carry away some of the custom carefully built up. This occurred at Oxford, with the One Day Flying Coach of 1669 between Oxford and London. Fortunately the aid of the Vice-Chancellor was obtained and very shortly a stern warning was circulated around the colleges:

> Whereas Edward Bartlet hath without licence from me, presumed to set up a Flying Coach to travel from hence to London; These are to require all scholars and members of this University not to make use of the said Flying Coach so set up by Edward Bartlet.
>                                        P. Mews, Vice-Chancellor.

Even in those days, having the right connections was a definite advantage.

# 4

# THE TRIALS AND TRIBULATIONS
# OF THE ROAD

'I was robbed last night as I expected', wrote Lord North, Prime
Minister of Great Britain in 1770–1782. 'Our loss was not great, but
as the postillion did not stop immediately, one of the two highwaymen
fired at him.' From this it is apparent that even the highest in the
land were not safe from the rigours and hazards of the road. We
tend to associate this troublesome time with the 18th and early 19th
centuries, forgetting that travel, roads and accidents have been part of
daily life for many centuries. As far back as 1342 a group of merchants
in Lichfield were attempting to bring to justice a certain Sir Robert
de Rideware, knight, who with other gentlemen held them up on the
road to Stafford Fair. They forced the merchants to part with forty
pounds worth of 'spicery and mercery' and although the town bailiff
led a posse against the highwaymen, capturing and causing the
execution of four of their number, the elusive Rideware escaped.

Since the Statute of Winchester (1285) some attempt was made to
police the towns by means of a nightly 'Watch' which was maintained
in all towns from Ascension Day to Michaelmas. The number of
constables involved varied from town to town and they were expected
to stand in a convenient place and stop all strangers. If the stranger
could not give a satisfactory account of himself, he would be clapped
in gaol until the next morning.

This was the fate of the Quaker, Thomas Ellwood, who in 1661
was returning late one night from visiting Isaac Pennington at Chadwell St Peter in Buckinghamshire. He was walking into Beaconsfield
and 'before I had walked to the middle of the Town, I was stopt and
taken up by the Watch. I asked the Watchman what Authority he had
to stop me, travelling peaceably on the High-way? He told me he

*The Master of the Hounds to Charles II being robbed in Windsor Forest by Claude Duval*

would shew me his Authority ... the Order which he had received from the Constables, which directed him to take up all Rogues, Vagabonds and sturdy beggars. I asked him for which of these he stopped me, but he could not answer me'. It took some considerable discussion before it was decided that Ellwood could sleep at the Constable's house overnight, before being allowed to go out by the back door and slip away.

*Members of the Watch on duty with their lanterns and staffs*

Others with sufficient money to offer bribes, found the members of the Watch only too pleased to accept them. In March 1668 Samuel Pepys and a group of friends were returning after a night's carousing, following a supper party at the Blue Balls near the Duke of York's Theatre. 'We met so many stops by the Watches that it cost us much time and some trouble, and more money, to every Watch, to them to drink ... but we came well home about two in the morning.'

The Watch were themselves at times, the culprits. In 1588 James Nycolles, John Copeland and John Armyn of Coggeshall, 'being appointed to keep the Watch, in the middle of the night, contemptuously and wilfully withdrew from their said watch and with a certain Daniel Turnor broke into the stream and fishery of Richard Benym

*The Watch and his dog from a 17th-century woodcut*

and dragged and fished the stream and took away the fishes to the value of 20s.' But the work of the Watchmen was important and at Chadwell in Essex, 'the petitioners have been lately enforced to keep a strong watch near the Whalebone in the great road near Romford by reason of sundry great robberies there lately committed' but it seems that 'the Constables and Watchmen there attending in the night being far from shelter are exposed to the violence of storms, tempest and cold to the great hazard of their healths'.

Also exposed to the whims of nature were the travellers themselves, for rain, snow, wind and flood caused both accidents and delays, so much so, that in extreme weather, the stagecoaches could not always reach their destination. To help the passengers in winter, the *Aylesbury News* of January 1837 reminded readers to 'To attain the maximum comfort which the circumstances admit, they should drink a tankard of good ale cold from the tap, and rub their hands, ears and faces with snow immediately before they start. This will produce a more lasting and agreeable glow than any other artificial means is capable of producing.'

The chief drawback to this remedy lay in the extremely early hour at which the travellers set forth, for in 1725, the practice was to start

*The foul roads of London*

off about three o'clock in the morning and travel until about three o'clock in the afternoon each day. A strong opponent of the coaching system in its early days, outlined his views. 'What advantage is it to men's health to be called out of their beds into these coaches an hour before day in morning, to be hurried in them from place to place till one hour, two, or three within night; insomuch that, after sitting all day in the summer, stifled with heat and choked with dust, or in the winter time starving or freezing with cold, or choked with filthy fogs, they are often brought into their inns by torchlight, when it is too late to sit up to get a supper, and next morning they are forced into the coach so early that they can get no breakfast.'

The snow and the cold hit hard, as there was no means of keeping warm within the coaches themselves. Even so, it was a great shock when the Bath Coach arrived at Chippenham in March 1812 to find three outside passengers lying in a state of apparent insensibility, but their surprise was converted into horror when they perceived, on a nearer approach, that life had been actually extinct in two of them for some time, the bodies being perfectly cold. This was a fate which also struck a guard called Nevill travelling on the Bristol Mail in 1806, and during the snowfalls of Christmas 1836 it seemed a fair likelihood that many others might follow the same fate. The snowstorm continued for almost a week, disrupting the coaches, blocking the roads and creating havoc. Strong winds blew the snow from the high ground into the hollows, changing the familiar contours of the land. Hedgerows were blotted out of existence; many trees had fallen under their snowy burden, and it was not unusual, when at last the snowed-up mails were recovered, to find them strayed far from their course, and in the middle of pastures and ploughlands.

The extreme amount of snow made the authorities in London round up carts and wagons to have the roads cleared and the snow moved was dumped in the country fields of the surrounding suburbs. *The Times* noted that 'Never before in our recollection was the London Mail stopped for a whole night at a few miles from London'. It continued, 'Never before have we seen the intercourse between the Metropolis interrupted for two whole days.' The night coaches on the Holyhead Road found themselves snowed up at Dunchurch, with one party crowding the *Dun Cow* and another the *Green Man*. On the first morning the coachman, guards and some of the passengers made up a poaching party, but had only two guns among sixteen of them, and they caught only one hare. In the evening a dancing party was held at the *Dun Cow* and the next day a group formed a chorus and wandering along the Rugby Road were entertained in farmhouses with elderberry wine and pork pies. I suspect they felt some regret when the next morning, the roads were reported sufficiently clear for them to continue to London.

For the seasoned traveller the cry was 'Give me a collision, a broken axle and an overturn, a runaway team, a drunken coachman, snow-storms, howling tempests; but Heaven preserve us from floods!' In this list of possible accidents consider that which happened to the Exeter

*The Lioness attacking the lead horse of the Exeter Mail Coach, 1816. (Post Office)*

Mail in 1816. It had just left Salisbury when one of the passengers noticed a large calf padding alongside the horses. By the time the hamlet of Winterslow was reached, it was apparent that the horses were extremely nervous, so the driver pulled the team to a halt. The so-called calf seized one of the outside horses and the noise and con-fusion was enormous. The guard pulled out his blunderbuss and was about to fire, when several men, leading a mastiff rushed up and stopped him. The calf was apparently a lioness which had escaped from a travelling menagerie! After a struggle the lioness was secured and the leading horse, which had been attacked, was purchased by the menagerie as an exhibit. This story caused so much excitement and interest at the time that two leading coaching artists, James Pollard, and Sauerweid, painted very effective pictures about the incident which were engraved for sale.

Coaches did not require extremes of weather to overturn or have other accidents. John Knyveton recalls, 'I did climb to the outside seat I had taken, and the Guard blew his horn and we drove off. The day was fine and I rather glad therat. But when we had covered scarce half our journey, and were out on the first marshes, the off leader shied at a hen flying across the road, and before we had scarce time to think what was afoot, the Coach lurches, and then tumbles into a ditch, the road being soft with mud at that point. The ditch was deep so none was hurt bad; but two women inside began to scream most piercing, being badly shook in their wits; and one gentleman was thrown clean off the road into the hedge and was hauled out Yr Obdt Servant and the Guard was all abroad in his wits.'

Not so fortunate was Sir Miles Hobart who died in 1632. A bas-relief in the Church at Marlow, Buckinghamshire, shows the manner of his death. His four-horse coach is depicted running away down Holborn Hill, the off-wheel is broken and the coachmen gone with the horses galloping away out of control. Coaches themselves were often liable to failure through lack of care, age, or simply careless assembly. Perches would collapse, wheels come off, axle trees break. The Bedford Coach broke two axle-trees in one day, while in 1805 a wheel of the Southampton Coach fell off and two of the passengers were injured when it overturned.

More unusual was the case quoted by John Copeland which took place in 1845. The coach was the *Salopian* from Shrewsbury. When the guard heard a sudden crash, on turning his head round he beheld, to his utter astonishment and dismay, about thirty yards distant, the hind seat of the coach in the middle of the road, with four of the passengers on the ground.' Nor was the damage always limited to the passengers. The *Annual Register* for 1759 records how the Worcester Wagon, owing to the bursting of a bottle of aquafortis (nitric acid) amongst the baggage, was burnt out, with a subsequent loss of £5,000.

One driver, dogged by fate, was William Upfold, known to his intimates as 'Unlucky Upfold' who was a coachman on the *Times* Brighton and Southampton Stage. A long series of accidents had constantly attended him from 1831. In that year his leg was broken, then soon after his return to health the coach overturned and he was again injured and idle for some months. In 1832 the horses set off without him and in stopping them he broke the other leg, and finally in 1840 he pulled at the wrong rein at an awkward corner of the road, causing the coach to topple over, and he was killed.

A more comic approach to disaster came from a coachman by the name of Davis, when on the Exeter Road he ran into some obstruction, upsetting the coach into the adjoining field. At this the sleepy passengers inside woke up and one shouted, 'Coachman, Coachman, where are we?' To which he replied, 'By God Sir, I don't know, for

*Fatal accident at Bellfield, High Wycombe, c.1895*

I was never here before in all my life'. A very pleasant group of passengers travelled with Colonel Peter Hawker from Hampshire to Exeter in 1811. 'Had a delightfully jolly party, and, not being post day, the mail stopped whenever we saw game, and during the journey I killed four partridges. When it was too dark to shoot, our party mounted the roof, and sang choruses (while I joined in them and drove) and in which the guard and coachman took a very able part.'

There were, of course, rogues on the road at all times, and Carl Philip Morits estimated that 'the highest order of thieves are the pickpockets or cut purses, whom you find everywhere and sometimes even

*John Cottingham* alias *Mul-Sack robbing the Oxford Wagon*

in the best companies. They are generally well and handsomely dressed, so that you take them to be persons of rank; as indeed may sometime be the case. Next to them come the highwaymen, who rob on horse-back often, they say, even with unloaded pistols, they terrify travellers, in order to put themselves in possession of their purses. Among those persons however there are instances of true greatness of soul; there are numberless instances of their returning a part of their booty, where the party robbed has appeared to be particularly distressed; and they are seldom guilty of murder.'

*Dick Turpin from a contemporary woodcut*

Some of the crimes were not of this magnitude, as for example, one amusing rogue who specialised in cutting through the leather at the back of the coaches and snatching off the wigs of the passengers. The tolerance of the highwaymen on the part of some of the public, even to the extent of condoning their crimes is apparent, both in the popular folklore of the time and in the actions of some of the more prominent people in the land. No less a person than Charles II once gave an audience to William Nevison, a notorious highwayman, giving the criminal a pardon, dubbing him *Swift Nick* a name used later in pro-clamations for his arrest. Similarly the Verney Family of Claydon, Buckinghamshire, numbered highwaymen among their acquaintances,

*Colonel Jack robbing passers-by of their jewellery, 1752*

and Sir Ralph Verney used his influence to save two highwaymen
cousins from their fate. He gave them money when they got out of
gaol and a wig as disguise to aid their escape,' finally obtaining re-
prieves and pardons to clear their names. His views were common
knowledge, and as John Verney said, 'Tis great pity such men should
be hanged'.

The problem of highwaymen taxed all the governments of the day,
and seldom was any ordinance or regulation able to halt the situation
for long. Fynes Morison noted that 'thieves in England are more

*Hugh Walpole being robbed on Hampstead Heath*

common than in any other place, so farre as I have observed or heard'.
Horace Walpole took these things for granted. 'I heard a voice cry
"Stop!" and the figure came back to the chaise. I had the presence
of mind, before I let down the glass, to take out my watch and stuff
it within my waistcoat under my arm. He said, "Your purses and
watches." I replied, "I have no watch." "Then your purse" he said.
I gave it to him, it had nine guineas!' As the robber rode away, Walpole
turned to a lady traveller and said, 'You will not be afraid of being
robbed another time, for you see there is nothing to it.'

In an attempt to foil these highwaymen, a new stage coach was advertised in 1808, running from Dublin to Cork, and as an inducement to passengers to take seats, it was emphatically stated that the vehicle was lined with copper and therefore completely bullet-proof. The scope of these robbers is apparent when, in one week in 1720, all the stage-coaches coming into London from Surrey were robbed. A gang which worked the Essex Road in the 1780s was so successful that they were able to rent a house at Romford where they farmed by day and robbed by night. When eventually the premises were located and raided, the Watch found 106 pick-lock keys, besides arms and other suspicious instruments.

Good advice to the traveller came from an ex-highwayman called John Clovel (*c.* 1603) who wrote his story, including the following comments:

> First you must keep secret your intention of setting out on a journey, and forego asking your neighbour, kinsmen and friends to breakfast or sup with you preparatory to your start; though they drink health to your good return they may be plotting to have you robbed. To detect whether your fellow travellers are highwaymen or no, take occasion to stop short, and see if, unwilling to let you go free, they do not slack pace. Ride rather by night than day with any sum you are afraid to lose. Then you will be free of highwaymen at least, for they themselves are at a disadvantage in the dark, and believe that none ride at night with aught worth stealing.

The value of capital punishment in supressing highway robbery was dear to the heart of Dr Johnson. John Knyveton recalls in June 1783 how 'alighting from my coach at a booksellers in Fleet Street ran bump against Mr Boswell, that shadow of the illustrious Doctor Johnson; then returning to call upon the great man after paying a visit to New-gate to see fifteen felons hanged. "Quite a fair morning's work, and excellent picking for Jack Ketch" observed the Scot. Doctor Johnson himself was quite outspoken on the subject of hangings. "Sir, executions are intended to draw spectators, if they do not draw spectators they don't answer their purpose." '

# 5

# PASSENGERS, COACHMEN AND GUARDS

'If' said the notable Dr Johnson, 'I had no duties and no reference to futurity, I would spend my life in driving briskly in a post-chaise with a pretty woman; but she should be one who could understand me; and would add something to the conversation.'

After so many complaints about the roads, coaches, highwaymen and bad weather, it is a great change to hear the other side of the story. 'Shall we journey in a barouche?' asks the *Blackwood Magazine* in 1826. 'Pleasantest of land carriages, whether horsed with chestnuts or bays. Tree and tower go swimmingly by, and whole fields of corn-sheaves seem of themselves to be hurrying to harvest home.'

Leigh Hunt gave his coach a life of its own. 'It rolls with a prouder ease than any other vehicle, and it is full of cushions and comfort, elegantly coloured inside and out; rich, yet neat; light and rapid, yet substantial. The horses seem proud to draw it.'

The pleasure of a journey was made or ruined largely by the position one booked in the coach, and the passengers with whom one travelled. The mystique of the coaching world is conjured up by the noise which assailed the ears as coach after coach rolled by. All coaches going north called at the *Peacock* in Islington. As they arrived, the old hostler, with a horn lantern, called out their names; *York Highflyer, Leeds Union* now *York Express, Rockingham, Stamford Regent, Truth and Daylight,* all with their lamps lit, and all smoking and steaming, so that you could hardly see the horses. Off they went, one by one and their vacant places filled up with new arrivals. The guard on one would be playing *Off she Goes,* on another *Oh dear! What Can the Matter Be* or *The flaxen headed ploughboy,* in fact all playing different tunes almost at the same time.

A Cockney and his wife going to Wycombe. *(High Wycombe Museum)*

As the coaches departed, rattling over the cobblestones, the horses' hoofs clattered in rhythm to the merry keyed bugles which the guards played so expertly and the passengers swayed and balanced on the coaches. It all added up to a great noise outside the *Peacock* at half-past six in the morning!

Along the road, some three hours earlier, other travellers would be rudely awakened from their slumbers by a *Boots* rendered ferocious by his own sense of hardship. The prospective traveller would have dressed with the aid of a light from a taper, which at each gust of wind from the broken window, threatened to extinguish, and then groping his way to the cheerless room below, waited, shivering and yawning for the arrival of the coach. 'In some half-hour you hear the faint wail of the guard's horn, mingling its tones with the still louder tempest, you rush out, and when half recovered from the first blinding gust of sleet and rain, you have the satisfaction of finding the coach full inside and out!'

To avoid such disappointment, the long distance traveller was wise to book his seat well in advance, in fact it was quite normal to make the arrangements at least a fortnight before the day of the journey. This could be done at the inns which served as booking offices, or if

# REDUCED FARES!!!

## MESSAGERIES ROYALES,
### *Rue Notre Dame des Victoires, à Paris.*

### NEW ENGLISH DILIGENCES TO PARIS,

*Every Morning and Evening at Six o'Clock,*
FROM

## THE WHITE BEAR, PICCADILLY, LONDON,

*Also from the Cross Keys, Wood Street, Cheapside,*

THE only Offices in London corresponding with the above *Company*, and where Places can be secured to

### PARIS. DOVER, CALAIS,

| | | | | |
|---|---|---|---|---|
| AMIENS, | OSTEND, | TOURS, | GENEVA, | BAYONNE, |
| ABBEVILLE, | CAMBRAY, | TOULOUSE, | MOULINS, | TURIN, |
| BRUSSELS, | VALENCIENNE, | LYON, | STRASBOURG, | MILAN, |
| LILLE, | BORDEAUX, | DIJON, | MARSEILLE, | &c. &c. |

Packet-boats are always ready, at *Dover*, for the conveyance of Passengers booked through-out; but persons wishing to stop on the road, are allowed to do it, and resume their journey at pleasure, without any extra expence, provided it is mentioned when the place is taken.

A NEW ENGLISH LIGHT COACH leaves Calais every Morning at 10 o'clock, through *Boulogne, Montreuil, Abbeville, Amiens,* &c. and performs the journey in *thirty-six hours.* The Fares by this Coach are:

From London to Paris { Inside ........ 3*l.* 14*s.* 0*d.* / Cabriolet ...... 3*l.* 2*s.* 0*d.* / Outside........ 2*l.* 14*s.* 0*d.* } *Passage by Sea included.*

Another ENGLISH LIGHT COACH leaves CALAIS every Afternoon at 5 o'clock, through *Boulogne, Montreuil, Abbeville, Poix, Beauvais,* &c. and arrives at PARIS in 30 hours. The Fares are as follows :

From London to Paris { Inside ........3*l.* 14*s.* 0*d.* / Cabriolet......3*l.* 2*s.* 0*d.* } *Passage by Sea included.*

At Calais, apply to Mr. *Tarnier,* Director, at the Coach Office, *Messe-Meurice's Hotel,* Rue de Prison, from whence Coaches set out every Day for the places above mentioned.

The Coach puts up at the *Paris Hotel,* Dover, kept by *Victor Poidevin,* and also at the *Ship Inn.*

There are also Coaches, three times a day, from the *White Bear* to
### DOVER, RAMSGATE, MARGATE, DEAL, CANTERBURY, CHATHAM, ROCHESTER, AND GRAVESEND.

NOTICE.—*Persons sending Parcels to the Continent are requested to annex a written Declaration of the contents and value; also the name and direction of the Person who sent it.*

\*.\* A Waggon to Dover three times a Week.

☞ *The Public are respectfully cautioned against the misrepresentations at the Black Bear, and their pretending to Book through to Paris, for which they have no authority, the Royal Messageries having no other Offices, in London, than the* WHITE BEAR, *Piccadilly, and the* Cross Keys, *Wood Street, Cheapside.*

*A stagecoach notice advertising reduced fares to Paris and beyond from London, 1835*

in London, in an extremely dreary and uncomfortable place where 'porters, like so many Atlases, keep rushing in and out, with large packages on their shoulders; and while you are waiting to make the necessary inquiries, you wonder what on earth the booking clerks can have been before they were booking office clerks. Your turn comes at last, and having paid the fare, you tremblingly inquire "What time will it be necessary for me to be here in the morning?" "Six o'clock" replies the clerk, carelessly pitching the sovereign you have just parted with into a wooden bowl on the desk "Rather before than arter" he adds.'

With the longer journeys it was normal to pay half the fare in advance, with the clerk entering the passenger's name and details in a huge ledger. Heaven defend the clerk who overbooked a coach, for the proprietor was obliged by law to convey the passenger by other means even if this meant a post-chaise, with a rate of ninepence a mile instead of the twopence to fivepence of the normal stage! For such an error the booking clerk might have to make up the difference.

If the passenger missed the coach, he lost the money already deposited. In June 1665 Mrs Pepys senior, having delayed leaving London during the Plague, lost her place in the coach and was forced to travel out of the city in a stage wagon. Once the fare was paid, there were still often further expenses, at the inns or in the form of tips to the coachmen and guards. In one trip to York, four different coachmen took over the reins during the journey, each of whom expected a shilling tip from each passenger, as well as frequent drinks at the inns.

The coaches themselves could be difficult to mount, and Hogarth in one of his engravings shows an extremely stout lady being helped in, or rather pushed in, from behind. A gentleman who lived in Edinburgh was under no misapprehension as to his size, and so always booked two inside places whenever he travelled to ensure his comfort. Sending his servant one day to book him as usual to Glasgow, he discovered on arrival that the man had booked one seat inside and one on top! A similar picture comes to mind in the description of another stout matron. 'Mrs Rochead's descent from her carriage, where she sat like a nautilus in a shell, was a display which no one in those days could accomplish or even fancy. The mulberry coloured coach, spacious, but apparently not too large for what it carried, though she alone was in it; the handsome, jolly coachman, his splendid hammercloth loaded with lace, the two respectable liveried footmen; one on each side of the richly carpeted step; these were lost sight of amidst the slow majesty with which the lady came down, and touched the earth.'

*Stout lady entering her coach at the* Old Angel Inn, *by Hogarth*

The main difference between the *English Mail Coach* and the *French Diligence*, writes one authority, 'was the number of outside passengers carried on the English system. The English have a delight in fresh air, and much prefer to breathe the pure air than be enclosed with a number of other persons'.

This practice, which was accepted as normal in this country, obviously was most original to the foreigner. Charles Mortitz in his travels also notes, 'they have here a curious way of riding, not in, but upon, a stage coach . . . he who can properly balance himself rides not incommodiously on the outside; and in summertime, in fine weather, on account of the prospects, it certainly is most pleasant than it is within; excepting that the company is generally low and dust is likewise more troublesome than in the inside'. This uncertainty about the status of the outside passengers worried a character in John Galt's *Ayrshire Legatees* (1821) who was 'obliged to mount aloft on the outside. I had some scruple of conscience about this, for I was afraid of my decorum; I met, however, with nothing but the height of discretion from the outside passengers.'

In fact the Baron d'Haussey notes that the place next to the coachman 'is considered as the place of honour, and is reserved for fashionables, and even for Lords, who do not disdain to travel there'. The schoolboys, as apparent from the *Tally Ho* coach in *Tom Brown's Schooldays* (1857), also enjoyed the freedom of the roof, eating oranges and shrimps and shouting at passing vehicles in the way boys do, 'But Lor' bless you, we gets into such rows all long the road, what whi' their pea-shooters, and long whips, and hollering, and upsetting everyone as comes by'.

The temper of the outsiders comes out in Dickens' comments in the *Pickwick Papers*. 'The outsiders did as outsiders always do. They were very cheerful and talkative at the beginning of every stage, and very dismal and sleepy in the middle, and very bright and wakeful again towards the end.' Of course they would be well supplied with thick coats and wrappers and protected from the rain with umbrellas.

The inside passengers got in at the inn yard, but the outsiders were obliged to clamber up in the street, in full view of the passerby, because there would not be enough room for their heads as the coach passed under the archway if they mounted inside the yard. Moritz adds 'The getting up alone was at the risk of one's life, and when I was up, I was obliged to sit just at the corner of the coach with nothing to hold by but a sort of little handle fastened on the side and the moment

*Nicholas starts for Yorkshire.*

*Nicholas Nickleby starts for Yorkshire. (Victoria & Albert Museum)*

we set off, I fancied I saw certain death await me! At last the being continuously in fear of my life became insupportable, and as we're going up a hill, I crept from the top of the coach and got snug into the basket. As long as we went up hill it was easy and pleasant. I was almost asleep among the trunks and packages; but how was the case altered when we came to go down hill; then all the trunks and parcels began, as it were, to dance around me, and I every moment received from them such violent blows that I thought my last hour was come!'

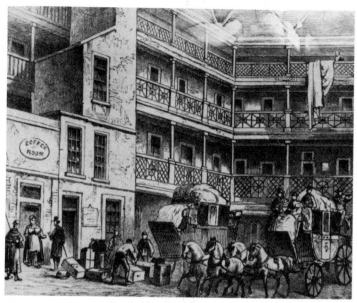

*Coaches loading in Aldersgate*

The basket, which was attached to the rear of the coach was used for luggage and parcels of the passengers, but even that was at risk. Sir John Fielding (d. 1780) the blind magistrate, gave warning in 1767.

To the stage Coachman, Carriers, Book-keepers, Tradesmen in general and others.
The remainder of that Gang of unhappy wretches who make it their particular business from this time to the end of Winter to cut off trunks from behind post chaises, to steal goods out of Waggons, from the baskets of Stage Coaches, boots of Hackney

Coaches, and out of carts which carry goods to and from Inns. Nothing can secure the Goods in Waggons, or the Baskets of the Stage Coaches, but the care of the Drivers, who should have them watched both on and off the stones, and the Proprietors of the several Road Waggons should have a Man at least on purpose to guard them five or ten miles out of Town.'

The stagecoach proprietors were, in some instances, responsible for the baggage they carried, but with goods over the value of £5, an entry had to be made in the ledger and an extra premium paid. When

*The Oxford Coach, 1792*

passengers were injured the proprietors were also responsible, although they preferred to cover the medical expenses and hope it would not go to court. In some cases it did, and sometimes the passengers won. At Salisbury Assizes in the summer of 1813, John Gooden claimed damages after the Auxiliary coach had overturned, injuring him considerably. Eventually compensation of £600 was paid.

In the case of the lady mentioned in the Annual Register of 1766, I suspect she was not so fortunate. 'On Tuesday last, a lady, through forgetfulness, left a box of jewels in the front pocket of a post chaise at Portsmouth, and before she recollected her negligence, they were gone beyond the probability of recovery.'

Obviously, with an unwieldy vehicle such as a stagecoach, much responsibility lay in the hands of the coachman, and his skill, good temper and sobriety were important factors for the passengers to note when mounting at each stage of the journey. Galt wrote that it was 'extraordinary what a power of drink the coachman drink, stopping and going into every changing house, and yet behaving themselves with the greatest sobriety'. Henry Fielding had another view, arguing that the coachman 'carries you how he will, when he will, and whither he will; provided it be not too much out of the road; you have nothing to eat or drink, but where and when he pleases. Nay you cannot sleep unless he pleases you should, for he will order you sometimes out of your bed at midnight, and hurry you away at a moment's warning; indeed if you can sleep in his vehicle he cannot help it; nay, indeed to give him his due, this he is ordinary disposed to encourage, for the earlier he forces you to rise in the morning, the more time he will give you in the heat of the day, sometimes even six hours at an ale-house, or at their doors, where he always gives you the same indulgence that he allows himself.'

John Macdonald, himself a postillion at one time to a private coach travelling all over the Continent feels he must put the picture straight, 'Now, before I go further, I shall give a set of men the character they deserve. I mean the Hackney Coachmen in Edinburgh, who differ from all men in Europe in their station. There is no stand of coaches in the street on a Sunday ... the coachmen dress like gentlemen and tradesmen, and go to church, where they have the first seat in the Canongate Church. No man may drive a coach on the streets till he enters into their Corporation, and have the coachman's word and whistle. By the whistle they call one another out of any house. The Coachmen always dress very genteely, the coach and horses are like gentlemen's ... in general they are more respected than in other countries.

The skills required of a coachman were often quite varied:

Wanted about Michaelmas, a coachman in a Gentleman's family, who can drive four horses, and ride postillion well; a single man, who must have had the smallpox, and know how to drive in London.

The coachman, in service or on the public coaches and hackney carriages was a man of position, respected among his fellows, in the inn-yard where he was generally surrounded by an admiring group of ostlers, stable boys, shoeblacks and other hangers-on. These all looked up to him, recalled and treasured his comments, and tended to echo his adages about the horses, often imitating his air and walk.

The typical coachman emerges from Washington Irving's *Sketch-book* (1819) as having a 'broad full face, curiously mottled red; he is swelled into jolly dimension by frequent potations of malt liquors and his bulk is still further increased by a multiplicity of coats in which he is buried like a cauliflower, the upper one reaching to his heels. He wears a broad-brimmed low-crowned hat; a huge roll of coloured handkerchief about his neck; knowingly knotted and tucked in at the bosom; and has in summer time a large bouquet of flowers in his buttonhole; the present, most probably, of some enamoured country lass.'

The factor of whether a man was a good driver depended on his ability to keep the coach going to schedule, and had little to do with the care of the horses. After an accident in a short story by Dickens, when four horses were lost, the driver comments, 'They were but horses'. Apparently the Spanish had a proverb which stated that England was a heaven for women but a hell for horses. The beasts were usually termed cattle, and often treated worse. They were worked so hard that their life span was generally three years. On one mail route alone, in 1821, twenty horses dropped dead in their harness. Apparently it was not the speed so much as the weight which was the problem, as loads of merchandise paid better than passengers. The early drivers understood little of the art of coaching, and were merely drivers. From early morning to sundown they whipped the same horses along the rutted ways, with intervals for mending the harness. When even the double thonged whip failed to rouse the poor brutes, the apprentice, a kind of cat-o'-nine-tails, would be brought into use and the horses thrashed with it.

The speeds they travelled seem very moderate by today's standards, but when in 1823 the drivers of the Colchester Coaches were fined for driving furiously, the actual speed was fourteen to fifteen miles an hour! Some coaches truly took on the name of slow-coaches. One driver, Joe Emmens, on a West Country route was famous for never turning away a passenger on the route, even though grossly over crowded, with parcels and hampers tied to and suspended from all kinds of hazardous places. This was not to foster his employer's business, as he pocketed many of the short fares himself, a practice known then as tipping. The custom was originally known as capping, and arose from the habit of the coachman doffing his cap when the passengers left the coach. One passenger innocently asked 'What do you expect?' at the end of a stage, and the coachman bluntly answered, 'Gents generally gives me a shilling; fools with more money than brains gives me half a crown'. Even the postillion and the driver of the private coach relied on these tips.

However, when a good coachman died, he was buried with pride in the graveyard. William Salter, Coachman of the Yarmouth Stage, died in 1776 and is buried at Haddiscoe. His epitaph commemorates his virtues:

> Here lies Will Salter honest man,
> Deny it, envy if you can,
> True to his Business & his trust,
> Always punctual, always just,
> His horses, could they speak would tell
> They Lov'd their good old master well.
> His up hill work is chiefly done,
> His stage is ended, Race is run,
> One journey is remaining still
> To climb up Sions Holy Hill.
> And now his faults are all forgiven,
> Elijah-like drive up to Heaven.
> Take the Reward of all his Pains,
> And leave to other hands the Reins.

As the driver hastened along the roads, the passengers chatted and got to know each other. Some private parties, when travelling, would agree to include a young lady if she proved charming enough. A certain lady named Mrs Fax, wishing to get to London urgently, broke into a group of five gentlemen who were drinking burnt claret in a kitchen. Being a handsome woman they gave the best place in the coach to her and she dined and supped with them each day at their expense. The leader of the group, Marmaduke Rawdon, was again travelling in 1656 when at an inn he met a gentleman and three gentlewomen of distinction, persuaded two of the ladies to join him in his coach, 'so dining and supping all together the party journeyed to London'.

This habit of drinking continuously has been referred to previously, and the *Blackwood Magazine* thought it time to clarify the situation. 'It is all stuff that you hear about eating and drinking plentifully inducing fever etc., during a long journey. Eating and drinking copiously produce nothing (mind and body being well regulated) but sleepiness, and I know no place where that inclination can be indulged less reprehensively than in the mail coach, for at least sixteen hours out of twenty-four. As for the interim, when I can neither eat or drink, I smoke if upon deck, and snuff if inside.'

The restless traveller who couldn't sleep through the night lived in a half-world of unreality. The coach would stop and a rush of cold announce the arrival or departure of a passenger, while the distant sound of voices were heard as they attempted to knock up the inn-keeper who emerged with yawns and excuses as the tired and irritable travellers slowly reached the coach. Wooden shoes clogged heavily around, and the horses' were heard swilling water from the tubs. Then the driver mounted and the coach resumed its way. In view of the dark nights and the state of the roads, it was a matter of amazement that the coaches made the speed they did on their night journeys. At times even the coachman got lost, and in one instance, on catching the attention of some rural yokel, found they could not understand a word he said and had they not found an old man who could understand what they wanted, would have been wandering around, lost, all through the night.

Anxious to escape to the Scottish border lands were the couples fleeing to Gretna Green. The travellers in a mail coach in 1821 were affronted by a chaise and four, the horses all in a foam, the postillions whipping and spurring like the very devil and a gentleman of very interesting and manly appearance on the box cheering them on to still greater exertions. The young gallant had not started a minute and a half from the *Bush Inn* at Carlisle when the father of the runaway girl drove up to the door. The passengers of the mail coach, realising the urgency, joined in the affair and the spokesman seized the reins from the hands of the coachman, and turned the horses and coach right across the road. The pursuers went after them, and a colourful scene ensued with shouting, curses, blows, confusion, blasphemy, and entreaty. However, before the father and his supporters arrived, the priest had rendered all further efforts fruitless; she had become a wife!

As the tedium of the journey crowded in, the passengers and coach-men would seek excitement or interest elsewhere, and Birch Reyardson recalls a road game they played. The passengers tossed for sides of the

*Post boys by H. Alken, 1822*

road, and totted up points with a donkey sighted as seven, a pig one, a black sheep one, a cat five, a cat in a window ten, a dog one, a magpie one, and a grey horse five. To add to the game, bets were placed, with money lost and won many times on a trip.

Robert Southey in *Letters from Espriella* (1807) imagines himself on the top of a coach as it bowls through Cheshire in the twilight. 'The sun was setting, and the long twilight of an English summer evening gave to the English landscape a charm wholly its own. As soon as it grew dark the Coach-lamps were lighted. Star light and mild summer air made the situation not unpleasant.' Following on such an air of nostalgia, we must agree with Dr Johnson that 'life has not many things better than this'.

# 6

## INNS AND POSTING STAGES

'The imposition in travelling is abominable; the innkeepers are insolent, the hostlers are sulky, the chambermaids are pert, and the waiters are impertinent; the meat is tough, the wine is foul, the beer is hard, the sheets are wet, the linen is dirty, and the knives are never clean'd! ! Every home is better than this.'

But that was not the way it should have been, for the smooth working of the stage system relied heavily on a good link-up with the inns on the main coach routes. Some of these were actually owned by the coach proprietors, while in other instances the innkeepers banded together to run the coach. So each was very dependent upon his neighbour.

The inns date back to medieval times, performing a duty to the Pilgrim and the traveller, which after the Reformation had passed on to the commercial inn from the monastery. In Chaucer's day, these inns were well established on the pilgrim route, and in his *Canterbury Tales* he mentions the *Chequers of the Hope* in Canterbury and the *Tabard* at Southwark. The legal position of inns and taverns was very precise, for taverns were licensed solely for the sale of drink and food, while inns solely for the accommodation of travellers. But many taverners sold ale and harboured guests without licence, for the penalty for disorderly conduct in un-licensed premises was apparently less than with a licensed tavern.

In England, by the 17th century, the reputation of the inn was at its lowest. John Byng, whose comments head this chapter, found it necessary to send a servant before him to prepare a room. Celia Fiennes, that intrepid 17th century traveller agrees on the question of beds, but was more fortunate in persuading the landlady to bring out her best sheets 'to secure my own sheets from her dirty blankets'. These then are different views from the account in *Description of*

The Blenheim *leaving the* Star Hotel, *Oxford 1831*

The Half-Way House, *between Knightsbridge and Kensington—a typical country inn*

*England* by William Harrison (1534–93) which boasts, 'Our inns are verie well furnished with naperie, bedding and tapisterie, especially with naperie for beside the linnen used at the tables, which is commonly washed dailie (the traveller) is sure to lie in clean sheets'.

Samuel Pepys was also of this opinion when stopping at the Salisbury *George*. 'Come about ten at night to a little inn, where we were fain to go into a room where a pedler was in bed, and made him rise, and there wife and I lay. Good beds, and the master of the house a sober, understanding man, and I had good discourse with him about this country's matters as wool and corn and other things. And he also merry, and made up mighty merry at supper. Up, finding our bed good, but lousy, which made us merry . . . .' The general condition of inns varied considerably, of course, from town to town, and the welcome the traveller received was also uncertain.

The coming of the festive season could be seen in the produce the coaches carried. This is well illustrated in James Pollard's picture *Approach to Christmas* (1828) which shows the *Norwich Times* coach drawn by six horses travelling through a truly festive snowy scene. It is loaded up with Christmas fare, parcels, poultry hanging on all sides, and a fir tree strung across the baggage which was piled high on top! The annual rush to get the geese to market was quite an event. In 1740 some nine thousand Norfolk geese were walked to London, which surely must have caused chaos on the crowded roads. Another time the Duke of Queensbury, for a bet, raced his geese against those of Lord Horford, but to ensure a good speed, the Duke's geese wore boots!

Whether one ate in the kitchen or parlour depended largely on the landlord's estimation of one's worth. Carl Moritz was ushered into the kitchen when he arrived tired and travel-worn one evening, but the following morning, when he descended in clean linen they showed him into the parlour. 'I was now addressed by the most respectful term, Sir; whereas the evening before I had been called only Master.' The kitchen in Smollett's novel *Sir Lancelot Greaves* 'was paved with red bricks, remarkably clean, furnished with three or four windsor chairs, adorned with shining plates of pewter, and copper saucepans nicely scoured that even dazzled the eyes of the beholder; while a cheerful fire of sea coal blazed in the chimney'.

John Taylor, who travelled considerably in the 17th century, compiled a collection of jokes which he picked up entitled, *Wit and mirth chargeably collected out of taverns, ordinaires, Innes, Bowling-greenes*

*and Allyes, Alehouses, Tobacco-Shops, Highways and Water passages.*
This was a kind of early joke book designed to help the shy traveller
throw in the old humourous comment when in company. Most of the
stories have a lewd and often familiar note:

'A servingman and his mistress were landing at the Whitefryars
Stairs. The stairs being very bad, a waterman offered to help the
woman saying, Give me your hand gentlewoman, I'll help you; to
whom her man replied, you saucy fellow, my mistress is no Gentlewoman, she is a Lady!'

*The ale house fire warms the customers as the dog in the treadmill keeps the spit turning*

The current gossip concerning the political scene did not go unnoticed. 'A traveller was talking what a goodly country Rome was, to
whom one of the company said, that all Rome was not in Italy, for we
had too much Rome in England.' While on a more morbid level,
'A poor woman's husband was to be hanged, and on the execution
day she entreated the Shrieve to be good to her, the Shrieve said her
husband was condemned and therefore must suffer. Ah good Master
Shrieve, said the woman, it is not his life that I ask, but because I
am far from home and must return speedily and my mare is old and

stiff, therefore I would entreat you to doe me the favour of letting my husband be hanged first!'

At times the innkeepers and servants were in league against the traveller. 'When he cometh into the inn and alighteth from his horse, the ostler forthwith is very busy to take down his budget or capcase in the yard from his saddle-bow which he passeth slyly in the hand to feel the weight thereof.' A rather fantastic story is recounted by Thomas Deloney in his novel *Thomas of Reading* (c. 1600) which describes how the guest room lay over the kitchen and a cauldron was situated immediately below the traveller's bed which, by the removal of two bolts in the kitchen ceiling 'in the death time of night, when the victim was sound asleep, they plucked out the bolts, and down would the man fall out of his bed into the boiling cauldron, and all the clothes that were upon him, where, being suddenly scalded and drowned, he was never able to cry or speake one word'.

An early broadside shows the concern which some travellers felt about the company they might meet. It implored the innkeeper thus: 'Although your house as an inne be open for all men to come unto, yet account honest men your best guests, ever hold their company better than their rooms.' It also advised the guests: 'Eat and drink for necessity and strength and not for lust. Use an Inne not as your own home, but as an Inne, not to dwell in but to rest for such time as you have just and needful occasion, and then to return to your own families.'

Contrary to what the broadside implied, inns were not only places of rest for the traveller, but also centres of entertainment for the villagers, meeting places for the Parish Vestry and often the venue for magistrates, members of parliament and other officials. As Joan Parkes relates, 'should the country gentleman wish to frame a petition for presentation to King or Commons, choose a Parliament man, or partake of a feast, it was to the inn they resorted. Was a meeting of the Justices convened, it was at the *Mitre*, the *Crown* or the *George* they assembled. There the young or convivial gathered to play shovel-board, the quack to vend his medicines, the pedlar to sell his wares. There too the bone-setter came weekly, on market day to set limbs broken in riding accidents or by other misadventures; and the show-man to display for a fee of sixpence his seven-and-a-half foot giant, his monster woman, or his groaning elm. It was the headquarters of the Recruiter who came to decoy the young and innocent into taking the King's shilling, and the haunt of spies sent by Government to learn

*Inside the Inn*

the disposition of the county or the intricacies of a plot. So truly there were fewer places in a small community more important.'

The *Ipswich Journal* of May 1753 proudly announced, 'to be seen at the King's Arms in Harwich, the surprising Dancing Bears, late arrived from abroad, who by an infinite deal of labour and training are brought to foot it to a violin, both in comic dances and hornpipes, even beyond imagination. Lest you should pass them by as commonplace, the report continues, 'the largest of them is eight foot high and dances to the admiration of all Beholders!'

But the prime sport, although severely frowned on by the authorities, was cockfighting. The Quarter Sessions in 1758 at Chelmsford were firm in their determination to put an end to the 'cruel practice of throwing a cock, and being desirous to discontinue such barbarous customs in time to come, do hereby charge and command all Chief Constables and Petty Constables, to use their utmost endeavours to suppress and prevent all such unlawful and disorderly meetings and practices'. This did not stop the advertisement. 'This is to acquaint all Gentlemen Cockers, that there will be a main of Cocks fought at the Kings Arms at Burnham . . . to fight eleven battles for two guineas a battle and five the main. Dinner at one o'clock.'

Another visitor to the village inn was the Recruiting Sergeant, anxious to enlist men, and painting a picture which gave a very rosy hue of the soldier's life. 'Wanted a few active well-made lads to compleat the gallant Corp the 19th Regiment of Light Horse in the East Indies. The Regiment is quartered in most plentiful country, abounding in all kinds of game; and the Men at full liberty to hunt, shoot, and fish as they please! They are mounted on the finest horses in the world, and each light horseman is allowed two Black Servants to take his Horse so that he has nothing to do but ride him.'

It was during the elections that the inns came even more to the fore, and according to an inquiry into the 1701 Maldon election, there were nine public houses where freemen who could vote for the petitioner were taken to be entertained. Several voters carried away drink by the pailful, sufficient to serve them for up to a fortnight. While in the 1763 election, some eighteen Chelmsford inns gave free entertainment to all county voters supporting one of the candidates. Several political clubs met at the inns, and one supporter of Parliamentary Reform in Essex, in 1779, walked from Colchester to the *Lion* at Great Bentley for a dinner in honour of Admiral Keppel. He was the hero of the hour, and in a letter from Thomas Barnard to Sir

William Lee of 20th February 1779, he notes 'We are promised another illumination tonight; Keppel dines with the City; his coach was drawn by all the blackguard Sons of Liberty that could be found, attended by a vast mob and a band of bad musicians playing *Hearts of Oak*'.

*William Hogarth's engraving of the election canvassing in the local inn.*
*(Victoria & Albert Museum)*

When the Frenchman Alexis de Tocqueville met Henry Hallam, the author of *Constitutional History of England*, he was most curious about this lavish hospitality at election time. Hallam pointed out that 'there are a great many electors whom he (the candidate) must send to fetch and when they have arrived they must generally be fed and housed at the expense of the candidate for whom they vote. He will not be able to get out of that for less than several thousand guineas.'

This atmosphere is reflected in the election in *Pickwick Papers*, for Dickens tells us: 'During the whole time of the polling the town was in a perpetual fever of excitement. Everything was conducted on the most liberal and delightful scale ... spring vans paraded the streets for the accommodation of voters who were seized with any temporary dryness in the head, an epidemic which prevailed among the electors, during the contest, to a most alarming extent, and under the influence of which they might frequently be seen lying on the pavement in a state of utter insensibility'.

At times the actual bribing of the electors took place over a meal at the inn. During the trial for bribery at elections for which Montague Williams was Junior Council in 1870, we are given to understand that at a dinner for his tenants at the *Dun Cow* in Wallingford, 'the invitation to the supper was accompanied by that which was likely to give the tenants an excellent appetite—the shaking of a bag of money in their faces. After the supper Mr Straight's health was drunk (the candidate) and such an effect had the bag of money, the meal, or some mysterious influence, upon the company, that, though it was composed of a number of persons who had always voted Liberal, all present were suddenly seized with the determination to support Mr Straight!

With all these events, meetings and novelties centred on the inn, the host or hostess, ostlers and chambermaids must surely be of exceptional character to cope with it all. Certainly they could be loquacious, 'Mine host, whether of the Garter or Star was a mighty pleasant fellow who drank and jested with his customers, making them pay for his jokes and potations.' But a much more worthy character was John Wigglesworth of Whalley. 'More than fifty years he was the perpetual innkeeper in this town. Not withstanding the temptations of that dangerous calling, he maintained good order in his house, kept the Sabbath Day Holy ... He was also bountiful to the poor, in private, as well as in public, and by the blessing of providence on a life so spent, died possessed of competent wealth.'

Nowadays we can look back with envy at the prices charged in the old bills for meals and lodging in the 18th century. A modest meal and lodging at the White Horse, Bakewell in 1789 added up as follows:

| | | |
|---|---|---|
| Eating | 1s. | 0d. |
| Wine | 1s. | 1½d. |
| Rum & Brandy | 0s. | 3d. |
| Rush lights, chamber fires, hay & corn | 0s. | 5d. |
| | £0 2s. | 9½d. |

But compare this with a meal taken at Brodie's in Newcastle in 1794, which admittedly includes the chaise:

| | | | |
|---|---:|---:|---:|
| Dinner | | 7s. | 6d. |
| Port | | 2s. | 3d. |
| Beer, Ale & Porter | | 1s. | 6d. |
| Cyder & fruit | | 4s. | 0d. |
| Servants | | 1s. | 6d. |
| Hay & Corn | | 4s. | 6d. |
| Chaise hire | £1 | 8s. | 0d. |
| | £2 | 9s. | 3d. |

However varied the meals in an English inn, those in a Scottish inn were something to be careful with. One traveller states, 'They have not inns, but change houses, poor small cottages, where you must be content to take what you find, perhaps eggs with chicks in them, and some lang-cake; and at the better sort of them a dish of chop'd chicken, which they esteem a dainty dish, and will take it unkindly if you do not eat heartily of it.' More happy was a young girl in 1804 who rhymed her views thus:

> Traveller frequently boast of the charms of an inn,
> But the *Blue Posts* at Witham's the best I have seen.
> The rooms are so clean, so delicious the diet,
> The landlord so civil, so spruce and so quiet.
> The servants all round so desirous to please,
> That you find yourself here most completely at ease.

The last line of the poem sums up the feelings of Samuel Johnson, who had something portentious to say on every topic. 'There is no private house in which people can enjoy themselves so well as at a capital tavern . . . there is a general freedom from anxiety. You are sure you are welcome; and the more noise you make the more trouble you give, the more good things you call for, the welcomer you are. No Sir, there is nothing which has yet been contrived by man, by which so much happiness is produced, as by a good tavern or inn.'

# 7

## PASSING THE MAIL AND CARRYING GOODS

The terms Royal Mail or a King's Messenger conjure up romantic associations of the Royal prerogative of Mail Coaches battling their way across the English rural countryside. The original use of the post was certainly for the Royal Administration, and it was in 1481 that Edward IV, then at war with the Scots, is said to have established a system of relays for horses. The post houses were twenty miles apart and despatches could be carried by horserider two hundred miles in three days. The service was originally restricted to the four great roads and in those early days its regularity was somewhat uncertain. An ordinance of Philip and Mary attempted to rectify this, stating, 'First it is ordayned that there shall be ordonnary postes laid at Dover, Canterbury, Syttingborne, Rochester, Dartford and London. Every of the Postes shall be bound to have alway the number of vi horses at the least, ij for the pacquett and iiij for goers and comers by post . . . Noe man shall ride post without a guide, which guide shall ever in his Jorney have his horne, which he shall blowe at the Townes end, where the poste is laid.'

The post was to prove of value to travellers not on official business, for by a proclamation of 1583–84, the public use of the *Through Post* was established at a fixed charge of twopence a mile. The posts, or posting houses, on the Dover Road were instructed in the 1550s to have a horn hanging at their doors, or a painted sign depicting a horn to show that they were post houses. As the use of the service increased, the postmasters were able to make their own terms (order of 1603) and the fee was raised to $2\frac{1}{2}$d. a mile, with a limitation of loads of not more than thirty pounds weight, with a speed restriction

*A messenger of the 15th Century*

of seven miles an hour in the summer and six miles an hour in the winter.

A re-organisation of the post commenced in 1635 when the four main posts were re-established; those to Oxford, Bristol, Colchester and Norwich. This was followed by a post to run night and day to Edinburgh which came into being in 1644 and later the announcement that there would be a conveyance of letters from London to all parts of the Kingdom.

Quicksilver *Royal Mail Coach passing the* Star & Garter Hotel, *Kew Bridge, 1835*

By far the most interesting progress was the farming, or letting, of the cross post by Ralph Allen, Postmaster and Mayor of Bath in 1720. He induced the Government to grant him a lease of the posts for life at a rent of £6,000 a year. This was something of a gamble, but, according to one source, he had a return in the region of £12,000 a year for the next forty-four years. Allen felt that while the through posts (those on the main roads out of London) were reasonable, the cross posts (those which linked the other towns) were few in number and some large areas of the countryside were not provided with any form of postal service. The system he set up was to last for more than

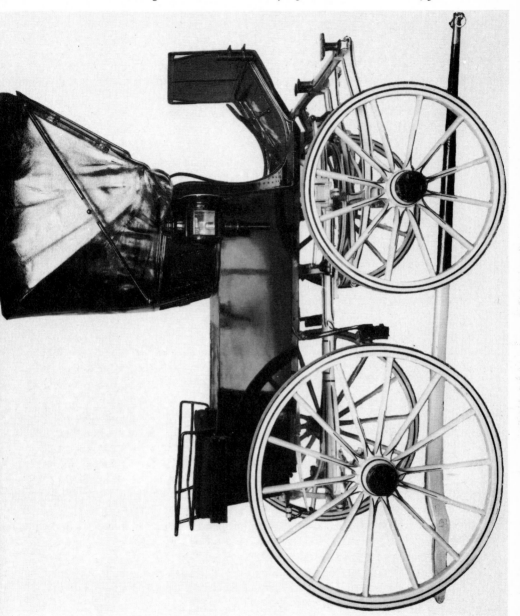

*Hooded mail phaeton. (Science Museum)*

fifty years and earn him fame in the couplet of Alexander Pope in *Epilogue to the Satires*

> Let humble Allen, with an awkward shame,
> Do good by stealth, and blush to find it fame.

A major step forward, which was to take the mail from the post boy on the horse to the coach, took place in the year 1784. To quote the prosaic words of the Postmaster General's First Report, 'One of the greatest reforms ever made in the Post Office was effected by the introduction of the plan of Mr John Palmer.' This gentleman was the manager of the Theatre at Bath, and he had noticed that tradesmen in that city tended to send letters of importance or value by coach, enclosed in a brown paper cover. Although the charge was much higher than if sent by post boy, it was conveyed with much greater speed and safety.

The complaints against the post boys were frequent, one example was related in the Bath Mail in 1770. '... did not arrive so soon by several hours as usual on Monday, owing to the mailman getting a little intoxicated on his way between Newbury and Marlborough and falling from his horse into a hedge, where he was found asleep by means of his dog.' As far as speed was concerned, it was widely noted that while the one hundred and nine miles between London and Bath usually took thirty-eight hours if the post jogged along, a post-chaise could complete the journey with travellers in one day. So the official report continues, 'The post at present, instead of being the swiftest, is almost the slowest conveyance in the country; and though from the great improvement in our roads, other carriages have proportionately mended their speed, the post is as slow as ever.' Even on the cost basis, John Palmer had established that the cost of post boys, and horses at threepence a mile was more than that of the stage coaches.

Palmer lost no time in bringing his Mail Coach scheme to the attention of William Pitt, who in 1782, was Chancellor of the Exchequer, but it was not until 1784 that the plan materialised. This followed an order issued on 24th July which announced 'His Majesty's Postmaster General, being inclined to make an experiment for the more expeditious conveyance of mails, of letters by stage coaches, machines etc., have been pleased to order that a trial shall be made upon the road between London and Bristol, to commence at each place on Monday the 2nd August Next.' The advertisement in the *Bristol Journal* assured prospective passengers that 'Both the guards and Coachman (who will be likewise armed) have given ample security for their conduct to the Proprietors, so that those Ladies and Gentlemen who may please to honour them with their encouragement, may depend on every respect and attention'.

The new service, which proved most successful did, however, meet with considerable opposition from the establishment. The former Post Office officials expressed amazement that 'any dissatisfaction or desire for change should exist', and the stagecoach owners were alarmed and angered by the introduction of a rival coach service, which not only promised to be speedier than their own, but which was also subsidised by the Government! The greatest opposition came, not so much against the scheme or the mailcoach service, as against John Palmer himself, and it threatened his precarious position in the postal service.

*Transferring mails to a post-chaise during the great snowstorm of 1836. (Post Office)*

In October 1786 he was appointed Comptroller-General with a yearly salary of £1,500 and a 2½ per cent commission on net revenue over £250,000. But after years of bitter opposition on administrative matters from succession of Postmaster Generals appointed by the Prime Minister, he was finally dismissed, with an annual pension of

£3,000. Some years later his son, Colonel Charles Palmer, obtained for his father an award of £50,000; but his true recognition lies in the service he established. Three mailcoach halfpenny tokens were struck in Bath, and one which appeared in 1797 is dedicated to J. Palmer Esq.; this is inscribed 'as a token of GRATITUDE for benefits received from the establishment of MAIL COACHES.' John Knyveton mentions the new coaches in his diary for the year 1784, referring to a young friend who 'by the aid of the novel first mailcoaches now introduced—which are said to travel at twelve miles an hour—and, what I will not believe—even at fifteen! that young man now flits about the country like a Will o' the Wisp.'

At first the coaches used were often converted stagecoaches from lighter private coaches, but in time Palmer approved a patent coach made by Besant and Vidler of Millbank, Westminster. This firm held the monopoly of hiring out all vehicles to the mail contractors, and

*The Early Delivery, c.1837—painted by J. Shayer. (Post Office)*

they charged initially 2½d. a mile. For this sum the firm collected the coaches each morning from the General Post Office yard in London on the completion of that journey, and took them to Millbank where they were cleaned and greased ready for delivery in the afternoon. In Britain almost two hundred coaches were mass produced to a standard design, and as Prince Kandaouroff comments 'spare parts were easily available and were speedily fitted in much the same way as motor car spares are today'. He adds, 'The travellers found that the mailcoaches, developed by private enterprise, were comfortable vehicles capable of very long journeys and high speeds.'

The coach was built with the body hung very high from patent springs which, contrary to the above opinion drew severe criticism from Matthew Bolton (1728–1809) the engineer. 'I had the most disagreeable journey I ever experienced . . . owing to the new improved patent coach, a vehicle loaded with iron trappings and the greatest complication of unmechanical contrivances jumbled together, that I have ever witnessed. The coach swings side-ways with a sickly sway, without any vertical springs . . . the severity of the jolting occasioned me such disorder that I was obliged to stop at Axminster and go to bed very ill.'

One of the chief complaints against the old system of posts was the frequent robberies which took place, and the Postmaster's report pointed out that in order to avoid a loss of this nature, people generally cut bank bills or notes in two sending each half by a separate post. This not only offered a better chance of keeping the money safe, but it ensured that the post office doubled its business in this sector. Although this new system seemed, with the armed guards, to offer a greater security against robberies, to make it even safer, the General Post Office, over the years experimented with, and introduced vehicles lined with thin plates of iron. A report regarding the Chester Mail notes that 'The bag of letters, being in one of the new-invented carriages, they could not get at them, and ordered the boy to unlock it; but he telling them he had no key; they damned him, and bid him drive on.'

By the 1830s the mailcoach was a common sight racing around the countryside and in June 1839 a report on the condition of the vehicles brought some concern. It found that many of the mailcoaches were dirty and shabby, in fact anything but fit for service, so when the tender for supplying the vehicles was advertised in 1843, full specifications were given. The length was to be 10 feet 8 inches and the height, over the door 7 feet 2 inches. The distance between front and back axles 6 feet 6 inches and the width of the track 5 feet $1\frac{1}{2}$ inches, with the fore wheels 42 inches in diameter and the rear wheels 54 inches. The outside was to be covered in leather and the inside was to be a drab lace lining with double crimson stripes with a carpet to match. Mahogany glass window frames and cushions stuffed with the best horsehair completed this elegant vehicle.

About the same time, William Bridges Adams advocated a new mailcoach which had a number of advances in design. It was hinged between the coach section and the driving section to allow a sharper turning section. The wheels were of equal size, which it was claimed would reduce friction, and the seat of the guard sheltered from the

*Birmingham Mail Coach in snow near Aylesbury 1836. (Post Office)*

wind. It is apparent that the Post Office did not wholeheartedly agree with Adams when establishing the standards, for they do not appear in the specification of 1843.

In the earlier stagecoaches, the coachman was the important person, but with the mailcoaches, the mail guards gained importance. They were appointed for each coach and would travel up to sixty miles on the journey before being replaced, and would then travel on the next coach returning to their home base. A mail guard's responsibility was primarily the letter bags for which he was answerable 'at his peril for the security, safe conduct, and delivery of them sealed'. The bags were locked in the mail box during the journey, and the guard was not allowed to leave them or even give up his seat to a passenger. As John Palmer had stipulated, he was armed, perhaps with a blunderbuss, a pair of pistols and powder horn and bullets. He looked after these with care, and he was also charged to cast an eye over the driver, and ensure that he didn't loiter on the way; also to watch the contractors of the service, to ensure the coaches were not overcrowded with passengers.

The guard was noted for the horn which he blew on entering a town to warn the posting house to get the horses ready for the next stage. On hearing the sound the turnpikes were supposed to rush out and open the gates so that the mailcoach need not slacken its pace. To give some importance to his position, the mail guard wore a scarlet

*William Bridges Adams' Equirotal Mail Coach*

coat and gilt hat-band, which no doubt gave him the necessary authority when interrupting the hurried meals taken at the inns, with the announcement that the horses were changed and the coach must be away!

The transport of mail and passengers tends to take priority in the histories of the roads and coaching, but a spurt of interest is often aroused when the name of Pickford comes into the story. The Manchester Journal of 4th January 1777 begins the saga:

> This is to acquaint all Gentlemen, Tradesmen,
> and others, that Mat. Pickford's Flying

Waggons to London in Four Days and a half,
Set out from the Swan and Saracen's Head.

The firm consisted of the two brothers, Matthew and Thomas
Pickford, and when they admitted Joseph Baxendale into the business
in 1817, the gentle procedures of a family business rapidly changed.
Soon they had close on a thousand horses on the great roads between

*Pickford and Co's Royal Fly-Van, c.1820*

London and the North-West, and the new advertisement informed
merchants that the 'Caravans on Springs and guarded, carrying Goods
only, left every afternoon at 6 o'clock from London to Manchester,
taking on 36 hours to cover 186 miles.'

As well as road trade, Pickford's became involved in canal traffic,
and by the time the railways began to threaten the goods vehicles,
the firm commanded the bulk of goods traffic on road and canal between
London and the Midlands. The rates that a goods carrier could charge
would vary considerably, and an interesting list in the Ipswich Journal
dated 22nd April 1758 in relation to the traffic between London and
Yarmouth gives a fair example:

Growing goods of all kinds @ 8s. od. per ton.
Weighable linens @ 12s. od. per ton.
Hops @ 3s. od. per bag.
Cheese @ 10s. od. per ton.
Spirits 5s. od. per pipe or 10s. od. per ton.
Barrels of porter @ 1s. 6d.
Wool of all sorts 8s. od. per ton.
Chests of oranges and lemons 1s. od. each.
Bales of leather 1s. od. per cwt.

This list gives a fascinating insight into the goods available for purchase and transport, while on the industrial side, some arrangements had to be made for the transit of ore or coal. In the Chesterfield

*Changing Horses for the Royal Mail, c.1780. (Hulton Picture Library)*

area, John Copeland records that a charge of 4s. 9d per ton was made with an additional toll of 4½d. per horse per trip in summer, and 6¾d. per hour in winter to cope with the long uphill grind. At times the contents of the goods wagon were very dangerous, and in 1776 a wagon loaded with three barrels of gunpowder caught fire and exploded 'by

*Posting chariot, c.1800. (Science Museum)*

which the goods were blown up in the air and totally destroyed, to the amount of one thousand pounds'.

The system of travelling post, that of changing horses at the posting houses, was introduced into England in 1743 by John Trull, an artillery officer, who obtained a patent for hiring out carriages throughout the country. The carriages, which were based on the French model *chaises de poste* were called post-chaises. They were light covered carriages drawn by two or four horses, and were driven by a postillion who sat on the nearside horse of each pair instead of on the coach itself as a driver would. In time the post-chaise was built with four wheels and the body enlarged to resemble the private coaches of the day.

*Royal Mail Coach. (Science Museum)*

These post-chaises became very popular and were frequently hired out at posting houses where fresh horses and a postillion would be waiting. The post-chaise represented, for its day, the ultimate in comfortable travel.

The development of coach services in America followed very much the same pattern as in England, except that for many years, progress was limited to the Eastern States, based on New York, as the great

*Henry Wells, First President of the American Express Company*

*out west* formed a real barrier in sending passengers, packages or mail far in that direction. There were, however, regular coaches between Boston, New York and Philadelphia in 1792 and in 1832 there were one hundred and six coach lines starting from Boston. About the same time the Baltimore and Ohio Railroad began carrying revenue traffic, with the first thirteen miles opened on 24th May 1830. Soon others joined the race, and by 1840 there were two thousand eight hundred miles of line in the United States. By the time of the American Civil War, this mileage had risen to thirty thousand, and played an important role in transportation during the war period.

It is against the background of this rapid mail development that the American Express system was planned. Henry Wells, one of the founders, commented that 'the Express system is due, in its origin to American ingenuity, in its development to American enterprise and in its organisation to American business tact and sagacity'. But the story dates back to 1839 when William F. Harnden undertook to establish a *package express* between Boston and New York. This was extended to Philadelphia, and by 1841 incorporated foreign express to Liverpool, London and Paris.

There had been baggage wagons for the transportation of packages and merchandise for many years, as there had been in England, and much went without cost in the hands of merchants and others who used to travel between the two cities. Harnden's venture was an attempt to regularise the transportation and put it on a financial basis. Henry Wells suggested to him that it might be profitable to run an express to Buffalo and Chicago and on to the far West—the terse reply was, 'If you choose to run an express to the Rocky Mountains, you had better do it on your own account; I choose to run an express where there is business'.

Adams and Co. Express had started up and planned a route from Albany to Buffalo in 1841. At that time there was no continuous line of railway or stages on the proposed route, so the express messengers were compelled to travel by rail to Auburn, by stage to Geneva, by rail to Rochester, to Lockport by stage and then by private conveyance to Buffalo, a trip which could take four nights and three days. These were at first made weekly, but by 1843, had become a daily service. One commentator noted 'the common road which ran 115 miles was in summer endurable, but most of the time simply horrible'.

There was of course no railroad west of Buffalo, but Henry Wells linked up with W. G. Fargo of Buffalo to extend the Western Express to Cleveland, Cincinnati, Chicago, St Louis and all intermediate points. The management was in the hands of W. G. Fargo, who, although he was able to use steamboats in the summer, had to resort to stages or waggons most of the year. In the winter it could take eight days and nights to travel from Buffalo to Detroit. The charges of freight was $14 for 100 lb. and for some time these receipts hardly covered the expenses. Among the more exotic merchandise, Henry Wells recalls oysters being carried from Albany to Buffalo at the cost of $3 per hundred oysters, and they caused much excitement on their arrival. Henry Wells moved to Detroit in 1846 as the express system

*Concord coach*

moved gradually further west, and this was only two years before the dramatic discovery of gold on 24th January 1848 at Sutter's Fort. By May of that year, the entire continent rang with excitement about the gold, and fortune hunters by the thousand made their way to California. The Military Governor, Richard B. Mason comments, 'The most moderate estimate I could obtain was that upward of 4,000 men were working in the gold district and that from $30,000 to $50,000 worth of gold was daily obtained.' The population of California, which was 20,000 in 1848, rose to 250,000 by 1852, and in the same period it was estimated that the amount of gold mined was to the value of $200,000,000.

It was the transport of the gold dust and nuggets which laid such a heavy burden on the Express Companies. Although there is no record of the exact amount highjacked during those early days, Wells Fargo & Co. estimated that in the fourteen years ended 1884, this firm alone had experienced over three hundred and thirteen stage robberies which netted the bandits $415,312. The cost in lives was sixteen drivers and guards shot in the raids, but seven stage robbers were lynched and sixteen others killed in gunbattles. In all, over two hundred and forty bandits were convicted and imprisoned.

These highwaymen were known locally as *road agents* and many have become famous through the efforts of film and television. Others who left their mark include Black Bart, a daring but friendly character who left scribbled doggerels at the scene of his crimes; Joaquen

*The Overland California Stagecoach*

Murieta, who, with a large band of followers, waylaid and killed many lone travellers and robbed stages in a reign of terror. When he was finally caught, his captors cut off his head to prove his death and exhibited it all over California for years.

The role of *road agent* was not always confined to men; Pearl Hart and Dutch Kate, who, in male clothes, smoked black cigars and swigged whisky with great gusto, were among the several women who took up this way of life.

In order to meet the problems these desperados created, Wells Fargo assigned armed messengers to their stages, and the merchants used many methods to disguise or protect their goods. One dust buyer put live rattlesnakes in the trunk which contained his gold, while another mining company melted the gold down into 700 lb heavy cannon balls. But as Wells Fargo maintained a strict policy of reimbursing shippers for each loss, there were at times merchants who wouldn't neglect an opportunity to tip agents off and so claim insurance and also get back part of the consignment of gold dust.

The drivers of the stages were the target, and their task was a dangerous one. John W. Boddam-Whetham, an English traveller, wrote, 'they may as a class be consummate liars, but as drivers of galloping teams, they know their trade'. Just as the stories built up about the highwayman, so the drivers attracted much admiration. On the death of Curley Bill in 1904 the papers reported, 'The dexterity with which he handled the ribbons over the heads of fractious horses, four, six, eight in a string, won him a reputation which extended throughout the new mining district.' Another notable driver was Charlie Pankhurst, a very rough character who constantly chewed tobacco, drank whisky and was noted for his profanity. When he died in 1879, some friends arranged an elaborate funeral, only to discover that this hardbitten old terror was a woman!

Heading the Wells Fargo force of investigators for over thirty years was James B. Hume, who was recognised as one of the ablest investigators of his time. The adage *Wells Fargo never forgets* was also never far from his mind, and once, having tracked a bandit for some months until he was captured and killed, Hume caused that text to be carved on the unfortunate bandit's headstone when he was laid to rest in a Virginia City cemetery.

An important aspect of the Express from Charles Fargo's point of view was the encouragement he could give to merchants and farmers to go into the new settlements on his routes, as he was frequently able to arrange or guarantee customers for their goods and regular and reasonable freight charges. In 1852 Wells Fargo & Co were able to reduce the price of Express freight from 60 cents per pound to 40 cents per pound, forcing their competitors to do likewise. In the same way it was possible for some of the companies to undercut the Government's postage from 50 per cent to 75 per cent and so gain a high proportion of that business.

Also travelling in the west between 1860-61 was the Pony Express, this was established following a telegram which J. W. Russell sent to his father on 27th January 1860. 'Have determined to establish a Pony Express to Sacramento, California, commencing 3rd April—time, ten days.' The proposed route ran from St Joseph to Sacramento, and covered 1,966 miles of mainly prairie country. It was divided into five divisions, each with a Superintendent. Over one hundred stations were dotted along the route with a main or home station at intervals between seventy-five and one hundred miles. Here a rider could rest before starting back with the return mail. Each rider covered the road between two of these home stations, changing his horse about six to eight times in each direction. They were paid $50 a month and given board and a room. Some 500 hundred horses were necessary to keep the Pony Express in operation, and more than two hundred riders were associated with it.

The main purpose for its creation was to speed up the sending of urgent or important mail, for while the mails moved by stagecoach, it was at a very slow pace, picking up goods and passengers on the way, and stopping when necessary for basic comforts. But with the motto 'The mail must go through' we find that famous riders such as Buffalo Bill (William F.) Cody and Wild Bill (James B.) Hickok, added much dash and adventure to the stories which are told of this venture.

As a footnote to this period, the notice pinned up in one depot was most telling. 'There are some employees who use freight as if they were born baggage smashers, and, of course, damage a good deal. Such men ought to quit Expressing and go cracking stone.'

# 8

## BETTER ROADS AND COACHES

In 1663 the Justices of Hertfordshire, Cambridgeshire and Hunting-donshire turned in desperation to Parliament for help regarding the current state of the roads. They reported that 'the ancient highway and post road leading from London to York, and on to Scotland by reason of the great and many loads which are weekly drawn by wagons, is become so ruinous and almost impassable, that the ordinary courses appointed by all former laws and statutes of this realm is not sufficient for the effectual repairing of the same'. Of course a number of parish councils and individuals interested in the roads had been saying just that for some years, and even a hundred years later the *Gentleman's Magazine* for December 1767 commented that, 'Statute labour is a burden from which everybody had endeavoured, and always will endeavour, to screen themselves, and on another Teams and labourers coming out for statute work (on the roads) are generally idle, careless and under no commands. They make a holiday of it!'

The only answer to these indictments was the creation of toll-roads, and following the 1663 complaint, the Justices in question were empowered to collect tolls from travellers on the Great North Road, and mend the roads with the money. Following the turn of the century other statutory Trusts were set up so that by 1770 there were almost five hundred and thirty Toll Road Trusts. By 1829, when an official report was made, it was revealed that there were 1,119 such Trusts, controlling a total of 19,798 miles of road. To do this it was estimated that over 3,783 Private Acts of Parliament were necessary at an average cost of £400 each. So the cost of establishing the trusts was tremendous, probably far in excess of the sums expended on the roads themselves.

To create a toll road, a group of local merchants, farmers or landowners would get together and form a body of trustees who could petition Parliament for permission. Once the Act of Parliament was accepted,

*The post boy waking the turnpike attendant,* c.*1830.* (*Post Office*)

the trustees had to set toll bars or a toll gate at each end of the length of road in question, and along it at intervals (in order to catch travellers who entered from side roads). They would then proceed to collect tolls from all travellers except pedestrians and those specially excluded.

There were many rules, exceptions and variations in the tolls system. The total toll was apparently doubled on Sundays, but the parson and churchgoers could travel free as 'any horse or horses carrying or conveying any person to or from his or her parish church or usual place of Divine Worship, on Sunday, or attending the funeral of any person who shall die or be buried in any of the parishes wherein the said road lies, or carrying any clergyman going to or returning from visiting any sick person, or other in his parochial care or duty' were excepted. So too were mail coaches, officers, soldiers and their baggage, vehicles carrying materials for road repair or carts carrying hay, straw or corn which was not for sale.

Although the purpose of the toll roads was to improve their condition so that the travellers would benefit, there was still continuous opposition to the charge from some quarters. The turnpike gate was a great nuisance, for not only did one have to stop, sometimes behind a row of vehicles, but one could also be further delayed by long arguments by some carriers with the turnpike keeper as to the correct toll. Also, if travelling at night, the gateman had to be wakened in order to open the gate. The coachmen in particular, were bitter about the high charges. In Worcestershire the charge for a regular coach in 1836 was between £6 and £9 a month, while for the private traveller, the cost of a journey from London to Scarborough, which is pencilled in the 1772 edition of Paterson's Road, cost the travellers £22 in turnpike charges covering nineteen stages. A journey to Edinburgh in August 1798 in which thirty-nine stages were involved, set the traveller back a total of £36 11s. 7½d. in toll charges!

When the Hull and Beverley Turnpike Trust was set up in 1744, the charges for a distance of 11½ miles were:

| | |
|---|---|
| Coach drawn by 6 horses | 1s. 6d. |
| Coach drawn by 3–4 horses | 1s. 0d. |
| Coach drawn by 2 horses | 9d. |
| Coach drawn by 1 horse | 6d. |
| A horse | 1½d. |
| Cattle per score | 10d. |
| Calves, sheep & pigs | 5d. |

By the time that the Essex Turnpike Trust Act of 1815 was passed, we find that the tolls were:

| | | |
|---|---|---|
| For every coach, Berlin, Landau etc., drawn by 6 horses | 2s. | 6d. |
| For every stage coach drawn by 4 horses licensed to carry six or more inside passengers | 2s. | 0d. |
| For every stage coach drawn by four horses | 1s. | 6d. |
| A riding horse | | 1d. |

The opposition mentioned earlier was not always passive, and some horsemen wouldn't hesitate to jump their horses over the gate, while in Somerset in 1749, the Gentleman's Magazine for July reported, 'On Monday the 24th at night, great numbers of Somerset people having demolished the turnpike gates near Bedminster on the Ashton Road, the Commissioners offered a reward of £100 to the discovery of any person concerned.' Much more significant was the apparent ceremony with which the offending gates were removed in a nearby county. 'A body of Gloucestershire people, some naked with only trousers, some with their faces blacked, destroyed a second time the turnpike gates and house at Don John's Cross, about a mile from the City. They bored holes in the large posts and blew them up with gunpowder.'

Again in Somerset, 'A huge body of Somerset people came with drums beating and loud shouts, and some disguised in women's apparel, and demolished the turnpike erections newly fixed.' Following this event, 'the turnpike gate was guarded with a body of seamen, well armed with muskets, pistols and cutlasses.' Things got so out of hand that legislation was necessary to stop 'ill-designing and disorderly persons who associated themselves together both day and night and cut down, pulled down, burnt and otherwise destroyed several turnpike gates and houses'. The sentence on conviction, formerly only three months' hard labour and a public whipping, was, following a spate of such events in 1727–35, raised to death without benefit of clergy!

The trustees not only had these toll evaders to contend with, but there was also the problem of the honesty of the turnpike keepers themselves. In 1858 a great hue and cry followed the disappearance of Thomas Hurcome, who was toll collector on the Drayton Turnpike Gate, near Daventry in Nottingham; also linked with him was James

*Private coach late 19th century*

Webb Atkins who kept a gate near Aylesbury, 'a dark man, aged about 36, slight, and strongly marked with small pox.' The documents relating to the affair indicate the following as lost by Atkins:

| | | |
|---|---|---|
| 1 month to 30 April | £46 13. 4. | |
| Part of 1 month to 31 May | £4 13. 4. | |
| 7 May to 31 Dec. | | |
| at £1 4. 7. per month | £8 12. 1. | |
| | £59 18. 9. | |

The Trustees at Aylesbury sent handbills to other Trusts through-out the country, and received information which led them to believe that Atkins moved on to take over the Battle Lake Gate, and was last seen in the fish trade at Ramsgate!

Most of the toll trusts started off with great expectations, which were not always realised. When the lease for the tolls at the Buckingham Gate was auctioned in 1825 'the said William Caless became the highest or last bidder for the same at the yearly rent of four hundred and seventy pounds.' But further investigation into the records show that for the year 1825–6 the total income was £384 7s. 10d. which shows an immediate loss, unless of course William Caless had some other business on the side. When the 1829 Report was issued, the toll trusts showed a total debt of £7,785,171, which by 1865 had grown to £9,000,000.

The true picture of how this happened appears in the annual accounts of the Trust covering the Baldock, Royston and Whittlesford Gates in 1828. The income for the year was £402 with an additional £114 raised within the parish (instead of undertaking statute labour); the expenditure was £321, interest on debt £153, and incidentals £13. As Sir George Fordham states 'thus the trust seemed solvent on its current working, but unfortunately it appears that not only was the original loan of £3,600 outstanding, but that £5,394 of accumul-ated arrears in interest had been added to it!'

Another thing the trustees had to do on receipt of the Act of Parli-ament setting up their Toll-Trust was to put the road in a good state of repair. Carl Moritz noticed immediately he came to England that the 'carriages are very neat and lightly built so that you hardly per-ceive their motion, as they roll along these firm smooth roads'. It was

# MACADAM'S SPECIFICATION

2" LAYER OF 1" BROKEN STONES.

4" LAYER OF 2"-2½" BROKEN STONES. (6 oz. STONES.)

4" LAYER OF 2"-2½" BROKEN STONES. (6 oz. STONES)

SUBSOIL.

*Macadam's specification. (Science Museum)*

*Telford's specification*

the practice to appoint a surveyor whose duties involved ensuring that the road surface was satisfactory. This could often prove expensive. £1,300 was needed to bring the Harwich Road to minimum efficiency and more to make it reasonably sound. The man appointed Superintendent General of the Road for the County of Bristol in 1815 was John Loudon MacAdam, who used his position to experiment with a new system of repairing and surfacing in his area. In October 1816 he treated a stretch of eleven miles of road between Bristol and Old Down in a special way. The experiment proved that three years later the surface was still, in comparison with other roads, in remarkably good condition. This was the result of meticulous attention to the correct grading and selection of materials together with care on drainage.

These were all points stressed by Thomas Telford, whose importance lies in the sound principles of engineering which he brought to road construction. MacAdam however, made further progress and created a waterbound dust surface, which with the slow grinding motion of the heavy wagon wheel, created a dust which, reinforced with lime, produced the binding medium to create his new surface. While the work was being done, there were complaints. Mary Mitford in 1824 writes with hatred. 'I do not know what good may ensue; but for the last six months some part or other of the highway has been impassable for any feet, except such as are shod by the Blacksmith; and even the four-footed people who wear iron shoes make wry faces, poor things! However the business is nearly done now; we are covered with sharp flints every inch of us ... So be it; I never wish to see a road-mender again.'

Another feature in the new roadmaking was the introduction of a sensible camber. MacAdam advocated a rise of only three inches over a road width of eighteen feet; the gradient used showed research into the capabilities of wheeled-vehicles. A gradient of one in thirty was considered satisfactory and used on the London to Holyhead Road.

Towards the end of the 18th century, the roads had improved sufficiently to allow the introduction of light weight carriages. These could be drawn by a faster breed of horses, and the owner-driver was turning more and more to driving as a pleasure or sport. For some years attempts to overcome the technical drawbacks of the older coaches had been made. We know, for instance, about the searches for a satisfactory spring by Edward Knapp, who in 1625 was granted a patent for hanging the bodies of carriages on springs of steel. Later Colonel Blunt carried on in the same field.

The elliptic spring was invented in 1804 by Obadiah Elliott and the C-spring replaced the elbow spring, changes which enabled the carriage design to change enormously. The wheel also received attention. In 1767 J. Hunt invented the method of shrinking a metal band tyre around the wooden wheel rim. The use of brakes was introduced about this period. Originally the method of getting a coach

*Town coach late 19th century. (Science Museum)*

down a steep hill was to insert a skid-shoe beneath the rear wheel, which then remained stationary and so halted the runaway movement. In time the skid-shoe was replaced by wooden or rubber blocks which acted directly on the wheel by use of a hand lever or foot pedal.

The chief carriage was the coach, the town coach with its sprung, agreeable form. This was a nobleman's carriage, a travelling carriage, luxuriously appointed and often elaborately decorated, exhibiting the family colours and coats-of-arms. An old coachman, realising the social value of these carriages advised the passengers, 'if you like to ride about for the benefit of public inspection, pray study Geoffrey Gambado on the art of sitting politely in carriages, with the most becoming attitudes, and choose wide doors'. The town coach was normally driven by a coachman from the box and light luggage could be carried on the roof. For short journeys the owner would use his own horses, but for longer travels, he would resort to posting horses. This type of vehicle was often sold to commercial carriage hirers, and so acted as post-chaises. Painted yellow, they were then commonly known as *Yellow Bounders* and could seat two passengers, were drawn by four horses, and driven postillion.

For the use of the town gentleman, Lord Brougham (1778–1868) one-time Lord Chancellor, devised what was to become the most widely used vehicle. John Wingate recalls how Lord Brougham 'asked his unimaginative coach builders, Sharp and Bland of South Audley Street, to design and build a refined and glorified street cab that would make a convenient carriage for a gentleman, especially for a man of such independence as one who carried his own carpet bag'.

*Dress chariot late 19th century. (Science Museum)*

As they weren't able to comply, the successful design came from the coachbuilders Messrs Robinson and Cook of Mount Street.

This first model appeared in 1838 as a closed carriage with little ornamentation. Broughams could be drawn with two horses, but in the town often only one was necessary. Soon after the introduction of the Brougham, the Clarence, named after the Duke of Clarence, came into use. This was midway between the Brougham and the coach and was affectionately known as the Growler. Like the town coach, the Clarence was soon being purchased secondhand by cab drivers and proprietors, and made available for hire. A booklet issued by the Glasgow Transport Museum, notes that at one time it was described as a Sovereign carriage.

The foremost extravagance in the range of open carriages was the phaeton, consisting of a very small body (often the single seat itself) towering on high springs above the light weight under-carriage. It was introduced in about 1757 and a print of 1776 shows it built sufficiently high for a lady of fashion to be shown stepping into the seat straight out of her first floor window. It was a dangerous vehicle,

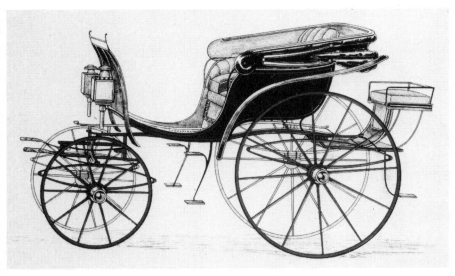

*Driving phaeton. (Science Museum)*

liable to overturn easily. It was frequently used at sporting and racing functions, and, as one writer commented 'there was always the chance that an accident might be fatal—an allurement in itself. And so in a very few years there was hardly a fashionable young gentleman in London who did not possess one, and drive about insolently staring down from his enormously high seat on to the heads of the crowds below'. But I think the description by Leigh Hunt sums up the attraction of the phaeton as 'the handsomest mixture of danger with dignity'.

During the 19th century the practice of driving in the parks created a need for a safer and more comfortable open carriage. This produced the park phaeton. These had very low-slung bodies with a folding hood fitted over the forward facing seat. It was drawn by two horses and became popular with lady drivers, who were often accompanied by a servant or gentleman friend as an outrider.

*The Victoria, 1889. (Science Museum)*

Variations included the Stanhope phaeton, introduced by the Hon. Fitzroy Stanhope in about 1830. This was also regarded as a town carriage for gentlemen. It allowed two people to be seated at the front with the folding hood available for shelter, and had room for two attendants to be seated behind. Another most popular type was the Victoria, somewhat heavier and usually driven by a coachman seated on a high box seat in front of the passenger compartment. Particularly noticeable was the very low slung floor which allowed easy access to the passenger seat. John Wingate referred to theories regarding the way this vehicle was named, one inferring that the Prince of Wales, seeing the vehicle in Paris in 1869, introduced it into this country, while another regarded it as the next step from the pony phaeton built for George IV in 1824. They were well known as Victorias by 1856 and in the form of a pony-phaeton were built by Andrews of Southampton for the Queen.

Heavier than the phaeton, but equally as elegant was the landau, driven by a coachman with two horses, or often four-in-hand. The seating allowed the passengers to sit opposite one another with large folding hoods fitted behind them which lay flat in fine weather. Should it rain, these could be raised and a glass window in the door made an enclosed carriage. The landau takes its name from the Bavarian town and was introduced in 1757, the original German design was modified

*The Landau, c.1890*

in 1838 by Luke Hopkinson and called the Britzka Landau, and the earlier C-springing was replaced by elliptical springs which allowed a much lighter body. It has been retained to this day as a state carriage, and the Landau in the Dodington Carriage Museum, built by Offord and Sons Ltd., was used by Her Majesty the Queen of Tonga at the Coronation of Queen Elizabeth in 1953.

The Barouche can be traced back to 1767 and is, like others in this field, more of a carriage than a coach. The Glasgow Transport Museum booklet rightly states, 'Quite superb and most impressive of all the landau-like carriages was the barouche. It could hold four to six passengers, and as their appearance was quite stately, several noble families continued to drive in them long after others had given them up. The beautiful boat-shaped body was suspended on massive up-standing C-springs high off the ground, and behind the body was a seat for the footmen, so essential in a carriage of state.

*Model of Landau, late 19th century. (Science Museum)*

Writing in 1837, W. Bridges Adams adds, 'of late years Britzschkus have taken the place of barouche, on account of their greater applicability to various uses'. It was introduced into England from Austria by Adams in about 1818, and within ten years had become the most common of all carriages. Made in various sizes, it became known alternatively as the Briska, or the Brisky. Noticeable in its shape is the length and straight bottom line, which was of additional value to travellers as they were able, when necessary, to lie full length in the carriage. It was suspended on C-springs and the body will hold four people with an additional two, when a boot is fitted behind. In wet weather it would only hold two passengers in shelter.

Other variations, the Droitzsche or drosky was a modification of a Russian vehicle, and based on the principle of a sledge. It was made chiefly for 'languid, aged or nervous persons, and children, as it is low on the ground and consequently easy of access and difficult to turn over'. Quite a different proposition were the two-wheelers, the gigs, traps and tilburys. These belong to the 19th century starting about 1800, and were in continuous use up to the First World War. The popular early ones included the curricle and the cabriolet. The curricle drawn by two horses, was used by Charles Dickens as soon as he could afford the luxury of a private carriage. The cabriolet which was introduced about 1815, had a shell-shape body, delicately balanced, and as it had a hood and could carry two people, it became a convenient vehicle for unmarried men to go out in at night, and return

*Painting of a gig, mid-19th century. (Science Museum)*

either from a dinner, or from the theatre, or opera, or Houses of Parliament.

This type of carriage always required two horses, as, having only two wheels, a great weight fell on the shafts.

The next and almost similar two wheeler was the Tilbury, which was a little more spacious and rather more heavily constructed than the Stanhope.

The term gig was applied to many of these carriages, and it included such variations as the Dennett gigs, Liverpool gigs and Hackney gigs. Although the gigs first appeared in Paris in the 17th century, the design changed little over the years, while the popular American variations, such as the Buggy, the Shay and the Sulky, took an affectionate place in local folklore.

The coach-builders had an important place in the trade, and the Coach and Coach-Harness Makers Company in London was founded in 1677 with certain builders strongly influencing the designs of vehicles. Notable among them was William Bridges Adams, whose *English Pleasure Carriages* of 1837 carried many of his ideas and opinions. He was particularly anxious to introduce equal-sized wheels front and back, and most of the illustrations in his books show the popular vehicles of his day re-designed on his *Equirotal* system. Samuel Hobson was another who can be said to have improved and remodelled every sort of carriage, which came under his notice. He lowered the height of the wheels of the coach to 3 feet 3 inches in front and 4 feet 5 inches behind.

The different workers in the trade are described in detail by William Bridges Adams. 'The body-makers are the wealthiest of all, and compose amongst themselves a species of aristocracy, to which the other workmen look up with feelings, half of respect, and half of jealousy. Carriage makers are entitled to a species of condescending familiarity; trimmers are considered too good to be despised; a foreman of painters they may treat with respect; but working painters can at the most be favoured with a nod. Smiths have usually been esteemed a very drunken race, men who work hard in a heated atmosphere have a tendency to drink more than those who do not, it is not surprising that some of them should become confirmed drunkards. A body-maker is considered a 'good catch' as a husband for the daughter of an ordinary mechanic; and the carriage maker excites much anxious feeling on the part of mothers . . . all these things of course create much jealousy and bickering.'

# 9

## HACKNEY CARRIAGES
## HANSOMS AND CABS

'Who can be a gentleman and visit in a Hackney-coach? Who can indeed? To predict nothing of stinking wet straw and broken windows, and cushions on which the last dandy has cleaned his shoes, and of the last fever it had carried to Guy's, or the last load of convicts transported to the hulks.' It was very fine for *Jehu* writing in the *London Magazine* in 1825 when plenty of vehicles were available for hire so that some choice was possible, but for those who needed transport around London in the early 17th century, anything on wheels was often welcome.

The Hackney appeared about 1605, but was not allowed to ply for hire, so it remained in the owner's yard until called for by the client. By 1623 the Thames Watermen had felt their inroad into the river traffic and John Taylor refers to the 'Hackney hellcarts . . . who have undone my poor trade whereof I am a member'. Up to that time the waterman had a monopoly in carrying the public, but in 1634 that monopoly was truly broken, for Captain Bailey, a retired mariner stationed four coaches for hire at the Maypole in the Strand. The drivers were dressed in livery and charges were set for journeys to various parts of the City. Soon other hackney coachmen flocked to the same place and set up their stand, charging similar rates.

Lord Stafford wrote 'everybody is much pleased with it, for whereas before coaches could be had but at a great rates, now a man may have one much cheaper'. As the number of hackney coaches built up, Charles I, who didn't view them with great favour, took steps to limit their increase. In 1635 he issued a proclamation which stated 'that the great numbers of Hackney Coaches of late seen and kept in London, Westminster and their suburbs were not only a great disturbance to his Majesty, his dearest Consort the Queen, the Nobility, and others of place and degree, in their passage through the streets, but the streets themselves were so pestered and the pavements so broken up that the common passage is thereby hindred and made dangerous and the prices of hay provender etc., thereby made exceeding dear ... whereby we expressly command and forbid that no hackney coaches or hired carriages be used or suffered in London, Westminster or the suburbs, except they be to travel at three miles out of the same'.

It is perhaps a coincidence that Charles I also granted to Sir Sanders Duncombe the sole right to let out sedan chairs, by right or monopoly for fourteen years. In his petition, Duncombe had

*The Cab, by Thomas Rowlandson. (National Galleries of Scotland)*

cleverly inserted the phrase 'in many parts beyond the seas, the people there are much carried in the streets in chairs that are covered; by which means very few coaches are used amongst them'. Although the sedan chairs had a period of monopoly, in 1654, an Act of Parliament was passed limiting the number of hackney coaches in London to three hundred, which highlights the fact that a considerable number were obviously plying for hire despite official displeasure. They were to be licensed at a charge of 20s. per annum per vehicle and placed under the control of the Court of Aldermen.

On the Restoration we find, in October 1660, that Hackney coaches are again forbidden to ply for hire in the streets. Even so, Samuel Pepys writes 'notwithstanding that this was the first day of the King's proclamation against Hackney coaches coming into the street to stand to be hired, yet I got one to carry me home'. And in 1661 over four hundred were on the streets of London, but as the streets were showing

*Town chariot*

definite signs of damage from the many vehicles, a tax of £5 was made, the income to be used on road repairs.

When the Plague broke out in 1665, the Hackney coaches were frequently used by people suffering from the disease. It was therefore ordered that where this was known, the coach be allowed to stand for a space of five or six days, 'till their coaches be well aired'. The Great Fire of London followed in 1666, and afterwards in the rebuilding, the streets were widened and more of the family coaches, either deserted in panic or sold off cheaply in a crisis, were brought into use. Taxes were increased in 1694 with a licence charge of £50 (for a period of twenty-one years) and a charge of £4 on each coach per annum. The same year saw a scene in Hyde Park when masked women in coaches insulted passers by, and so produced the prohibition against coaches entering the Park.

William Congreve, the poet and dramatist, was appointed Commissioner for Licensing Hackney coaches in 1695, at a salary of £100 a year, a post he held until 1707. Another writer, Dean Swift, was the cause of one driver's annoyance, for when Swift and some other clerics arrived at his house, the coachman opened the door and let down the steps. Dean Swift alighted, very dignified in his black robes; after came another equally black and dignified, then a third, followed

*Wheeled sedan chair, 19th century*

by a fourth. The coachman, who recollected taking up no greater number, was about to put up the steps, when another clergyman descended. After giving way to this other, he proceeded with great confidence to toss them up, when another appeared. The coachman cried out, 'The Devil! the Devil!' and prepared to run away, when they all burst into laughter. They had gone round as they descended, and got in again at the other door.

It was probably a such similar incident which caused some drivers take retaliatory action. 'Whereas I, William Ford, late driver of an Hackney Coach No. 694, did refuse to carry a gentleman, and did also grossly abuse him, for this I was fined thirty shillings by the Commissioners. I then most wickedly and falsely swore an assault against and had the same gentleman carried before Sir John Fielding . . . I therefore voluntary insert this caution to other hackney coachmen, who will know that it is from the home of forgiveness, which they often meet, that they venture so daringly to abuse and insult their fare.'

It was Sir John Fielding, the blind magistrate, who warned the tradesmen and coachmen against thefts from vehicles, drawing particular attention to the Hackney coach.

'As it is common for Persons on their Arrival in Town to take a Hackney Coach when they come on the Stones, in the Boot of which they generally deposit their luggage, they should be cautious never to send the Coachman from his Boot, for if he be absent a Minute his Fare will be in great danger of losing his Property, by some of the above offenders who attend at the Inns at the entrance of the Town, in order to follow Hackney Coaches to the Places where they set down or stop, to watch an Opportunity to plunder.'

The warning was timely, as the number of vehicles licensed to ply or stand for hire in the street had, by 1768, risen to a thousand, but of these only one hundred and seventy-five were allowed to ply for hire on Sundays. The trade was becoming organised, as other men were licensed to look after and water the horses while the coachmen rested, ate, or waited for fares. These were called *watermen, caddies* or *cads*, and they were recognisable from the brass label around their necks. They also opened the doors of the coaches for the passengers and lowered the steps, for this the coachman paid the caddy a half-penny.

These coachmen tended to have rather independent natures. When the Coronation of George III was announced, the sedan chair-men and the Hackney coach drivers got together and decided not to take their vehicles on the road unless they could charge higher fares on that festive day. This caused much consternation, as many had intended to use Hackney coaches to take them to Westminster to witness the ceremony or the procession. The Privy Council ordered all sedan chairmen and Hackney coachmen to be at their stands by four o'clock in the morning on Coronation Day, and warned that over-charging would incur maximum punishment.

At first the opinion was against turning out, so defying the official order, but moderate council won the day and the drivers turned out with their vehicles and in general received more recompense than was expected.

In time the vehicles were designed to suit the type of custom they were dealing with, and early in the 19th century, a more lightly constructed *chariot* was built which could carry two passengers inside and another on the box seat. The coachman often rode the nearside horse, and later began to sit on the box seat. By 1814 over two hundred Hackney chariots were licensed in London alone. In case

*Family travelling coach (1817), also called a 'park coach' or 'drag'*

it should be thought that the Hackney carriage or the sedan chair was to be found only in the capital, evidence to the contrary shows they were used in other towns throughout the kingdom..

A book of regulations dated 1822 was issued at Exeter governing the use of sedan chairs in that city, and similar regulations related to the Hackney coach. Originally the sedan chair was found to be most manoeuvrable in the narrow streets, but as rebuilding took place the Hackney carriages or chariots began to gain in popularity until by 1821 only one sedan chair stand remained in London.

Conditions for the use of Hackney carriages in Bristol were laid down by the City Council in 1826. They decreed that where more than three passengers were carried, the fare could be increased by a quarter for each extra person. The rate beyond the set fares to be one shilling

*The* Coffin *Cab, from a drawing by Cruikshank*

a mile and sixpence a half mile. The rules also allowed double rates after midnight, and hourly rates based on a speed of not less than four miles per hour. At Exeter the Hackney coachmen were required, between 9.00 a.m. and 11.00 p.m. to remain at the stands unless actually conveying passengers, a working day of fourteen hours!

The coach proprietors were therefore in a position where they were open to blackmail. 'A fellow would stroll into a hackney coachyard and chat with the proprietor, finally asking for a half-sovereign, which was usually given.' If the request wasn't met, a summons would follow a few days later, for some minor irregularity regarding the driver, the vehicles or horses, and this would continue until the payments were started again. The part of informer could be quite lucrative, as he received half of every fine imposed due to his report.

Then followed the new fad the cabriolet, a style of carriage already popular on the Continent, which arrived in London in 1805 under the auspices of Messrs. Bradshaw & Rotch. Nine cabriolets were obtained to serve the outskirts of London, as the Hackney coaches still had a monopoly of the City itself. It was not until 1823 that twelve fully licensed cabriolets built by David Davies, were placed for hire in honour of his Majesty's Birthday!

A feature of the cabriolet was the elegant bodywork and beautifully finished leather hood. A small platform or seat was fitted at the rear which allowed a groom to hang on in the private carriage. There was a tendency to choose a small groom and dress him in a striped waist-coat, causing him to be called a *Tiger*. Sometimes the driver's seat was built out on the offside between the body of the vehicle and the wheel. This seat was topped with a hood and because of its tall, thin shape, resembled a coffin on end, thereby earning the nickname *Coffin-cabs*. The fare, at eightpence a mile with fourpence for each additional half mile, meant they were cheaper, and due to their size, quicker than the hackney carriage. Of course there were drawbacks. If the horse fell, or stopped abruptly the helpless passenger pitched forward and could easily shoot over the head of the horse!

Charles Dickens wrote, 'Cabs are very well in cases of expedition, when it's a matter of neck or nothing, life or death, your temporary home or your long one, a hackney cab has always been a hackney cab, from its first entry into public life, whereas a hackney coach is a remnant of past gentility, a victim of fashion, a hanger-on of an old English family.' The picture of the rivalry between the cabdriver and the hackney coachman is further evoked by Dickens in *Sketches by*

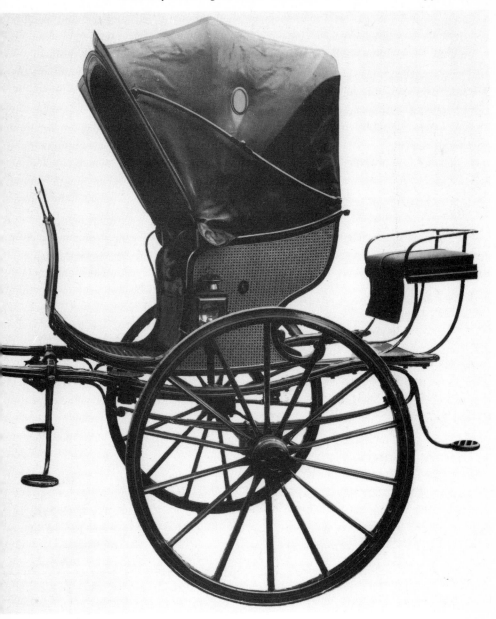

*Hooded buggy with rumble seat*

*Boz*, when describing the wakening moments of the great city. 'Cabs, with trunks and bandboxes between the driver's legs and outside the apron, rattle briskly up and down the streets on their way to the coach offices or steam packet wharfs, and the cab drivers and hackney coachmen who are on the stand, polish up the ornamental part of the dingy vehicles, the former wondering how people can prefer "them wild beast carivans of homnibuses to a regular cab with a fast trotter", and the latter admiring how people can trust their necks into one of them crazy cabs, when they can have a "spectable 'ackney cotche with a pair of 'orses as von't run away with no von." '

The popularity of the cabs was slowly growing, but due to the monopoly of hackney coaches, this was nowhere near the speed of growth taking place on the Continent. In London, in 1832, when the total number of cabs was one hundred and sixty five, in Paris where they originated, there were over two thousand five hundred.

About this time a new cab invented by William Boulnois was introduced with a back door which carried two passengers sitting opposite each other. The driver sat atop the roof, but this proved rather dangerous, and the back door frequently enabled passengers to slip out without paying their fare!

In 1834, another inventor, Joseph Hansom, patented a style of cab with a solid roof instead of a folding cover; the driver sat on a seat fitted on top and the carriage was hung between two giant seven foot wheels. Hansom was financed by William Boulnois, but this design was also not very practical. It was only when modifications were made by John Chapman, secretary of the Safety Cabriolet and Two-Wheeler Carriage Company, that the design was successful. Chapman made the wheels smaller, the driver sat on a seat at the back, behind the body of the cab, it had windows on each side and an entrance for two passengers in the front. In fact only the original name was retained. These new cabs were soon on the streets and painted in a similar way to the Hansom cabs. One feature with a comic element was the small trapdoor in the roof, through which the passenger could speak to the driver.

Some of the vehicles still plying for hire in 1836 were Hackney coaches, cabriolets and the back-door cabs, but the proprietors, seeing the great successes of Chapman's cab, made attempts to build and run similar vehicles. They even had them painted identically and lettered *Not Hansom's Patent Safety*, hoping this would delude the public and still keep them from being accused of infringing the patent.

*Mr. Pickwick travels in a Hackney. (Victoria & Albert Museum)*

The first four-wheeler cab appeared about the same time as the Chapman cab. It was made by David Davies, and eventually became known as the *Clarence* or more familiarly as *The Growler*. This was most popular with the elderly or respectable clientele who considered the Hansoms rather fast and disreputable. From time to time the regulations and the rates for mileage were changed and grumbles from the public or the cabmen were ever present. Things came to a head when, in 1853, the fare for cabs was reduced from eightpence a mile to sixpence a mile or any part of a mile. This so enraged the cabmen

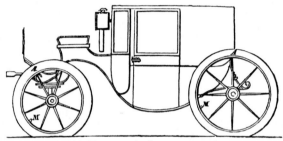

R. W. THOMSON'S BROUGHAM, 1846.

| *Weight of carriage with its load 15 cwt. | | |
|---|---|---|
| On paved streets the common wheels require a force of . . . . . . | 48 lbs. | |
| The patent wheels . . . . . | | 28 lbs. |
| On clean, smooth, hard, Macadamised road the common wheels require a force of . | 40 lbs. | |
| The patent wheels . . . . . | | 25 lbs. |
| On broken granite newly laid down the common wheels require a force of . . . | 130 lbs. | |
| The patent wheels . . . . . | | 40 lbs. |

\* Extract from the *Mechanics Magazine*, 1849, Vol. 50.

*The Brougham, modified by R. W. Thomas in 1846*

that when the Parliament rose in the evening of 26th July they withdrew their vehicles so that the Members of Parliament rushing out after a critical division, found to their horror that all they could see were the cabs disappearing empty into the distance! The next morning not a cab was on the streets, as the cabmen were on strike!

This situation lasted for four days, but then, as unlicensed cabs were busily picking up their custom without any interference from the police, they returned to work. However, they did eventually get the new fares reviewed.

At the high tide of popularity of the hired carriage in London in the mid-19th century, we find that in 1860, there were 4,300 licensed cabs and 200 cabstands. By 1900 the figures had shot up, so that statistics show there were 7,531 licensed two-wheel cabs, and 3,721 fourwheelers, a total of 11,252 cabs, 13,201 cab drivers and 2,782 proprietors.

The world of coaching had its own language, so we learn that an empty coach was known as a *mad woman*, that a passenger who slipped out of the coach without paying was a *bilker*; a passenger not on the bill *a shoulder stick* or a *short one*. With the practice of tipping, those who gave small tips were *scaly ones*, and no tip was termed *tipping the double* while a pretty girl was, of course, *a pretty bit of muslin*. Parts of the coach carried slang terms. The coach was often called a *drag*, the reins were popularly the *ribbons* and the horses termed, quite often correctly as *cattle*.

Certain cabmen also had their peculiar names, a well set up one was known as *Nonpareil*, and Henry Moore, writing in 1902 refers to such characters as *Engineer Charly* or *Father Christmas*, *Australian Jack*, and the expressive *Rhoderic Dhu*. He also draws attention to the names given to the proprietors; to *Pious Tommy* who wouldn't allow swearing in his yard; *Jack the Giant Killer* at only 5 feet 2 inches high; or *Boozy Bill* the teetotaller, and among the women was *Fairy Emma* who was so stout she could hardly walk.

The characters among the passengers were many, some sad, some humorous and some feared, such as Mrs Prodgers. She had such an extensive knowledge of the streets of London, of the cab regulations and the mileages concerned, that few dared question her fare without finding a summons laid against them. 'After a time, she became so dreaded that the warning cry of *Mother Prodgers* was sufficient to send every cab within hail dashing away up side streets to escape her!'

# 10

## THE OMNIBUS AND THE ARRIVAL
## OF THE RAILWAYS

On the morning of 18th March 1662, a great crowd gathered at the Luxembourg in Paris, when, with such ceremony and fine speeches, the first omnibus set off on its journey. The coachmen were presented with long blue coats with the city arms embroidered on the front in bright colours. The scheme was the result of co-operation between Blaise Pascal, the Duc de Rouanes, and others, after permission had been given by Louis XIV.

The excitement was considerable. People crowded round and the seven vehicles which were made to carry eight passengers each, had no lack of fares. At the beginning of every journey the struggle to get into the coach was repeated. Paris, in short, went mad over its *carrosses a cinq sous* as they were called. Within four months a further four routes were opened, but then suddenly the fashion died, as did the profits, and as Pascal died soon after, the whole project was discontinued.

A century and a half elapsed before anyone was foolhardy enough to repeat the experiment, and strange though it may seem, it was in Paris that the new omnibuses, as they were called, ran again. These were now larger, carrying sixteen to eighteen passengers and again had success from the moment of their revival in 1819. Watching this success was an English coachbuilder by the name of George Shillibeer who wrote in 1828 to the Treasury in England, 'Your memorialist has no doubt but what your Lordships have heard of the new public vehicles called Omnibus recently established at Paris and authorised by an ordonnaunce from the Prefecture of Police to convey passengers without luggage to and from the barriers of Paris at the moderate charge of five sous or 2½d. for a course of about one mile and a half English.

'Your memorialist . . . contemplating establishing them in London under the more English name of Economist . . . It is with the strongest impression of their utility here, where the expense of conveyance is so high that the industrious part of the community are obliged to walk, that your memorialist most humbly begs to solicit your Lordship's

*Shillibeer's Omnibus*

sanction to work three carriages upon the most frequented routes of the Metropolis. . . .'

Unfortunately the pressure to retain the Hackney carriage monopoly over these routes caused the Lords of the Treasury to refuse Shillibeer's request, so he tried it out along New Road from Paddington to the Bank, a route not subject to the law. The service started on 4th July 1829 and the name Omnibus was retained. The advertisement informed the travelling public that 'the superiority of this carriage over the ordinary stage coaches for comfort and safety must be obvious, all the passengers being inside and the fare charged from Paddington to the Bank being one shilling, and from Islington to Bank or Paddington, sixpence'.

The new conductors were dressed in dark velvet suits, and 'as far as politeness was concerned were all that could be desired'. Henry Moore reports, 'unfortunately they became possessed of the belief, not yet quite extinct, that to rob an omnibus proprietor was no sin.' When

Shillibeer noticed a sharp falling off of receipts, he made checks of the number of persons travelling on the omnibus and discovered that at least two conductors between them were pocketing over £20 a week!

Despite all this, Shillibeer prospered for some time, having twelve omnibuses on the road within nine months, and of a design so useful that the Post Office used four similar vehicles to transport their post-

*To Brighton and Back for 3s 6d., by Charles Rossiter. (City of Birmingham)*

men to different parts of London. Other routes were opened, until by May 1830 up to thirty-nine omnibuses were running in London. In 1832, the *Stage Carriage Act* did away with the monopoly formerly held by the Hackney carriages, and so opened up the whole of the centre of London to the rival activities of various omnibus proprietors.

Besides his London routes, Shillibeer ran a 'new patent improved diligence' every day to Brighton, and the vehicles, which were drawn by three horses, took six hours. The charge was sixteen shillings for the omnibus class, and ten shillings for the exterior passengers. But as the competition for the customers built up in London, and following a number of disappointments and business failures, George Shillibeer found himself committed to Fleet Prison for debt, where he stayed

for several months. After his release he changed his profession, de-
signing a new type of funeral carriage, which enabled him to set up in
the City Road as an undertaker, with considerably more success. A
very good example of a Shillibeer hearse stands in the Folk museum
at Shibden Hall, near Halifax, and its glazed and carved elegance
must have added considerably to the dignity of these solemn occasions.

The omnibuses now spread to other cities, and R. B. Dockray

*William Bridges Adams' Equirotal Omnibus*

describes in his diary the omnibuses of Liverpool as 'much superior
to those in London; or indeed anywhere else that I have seen; they
are so broad that the conductor can walk between people's knees
without inconveniencing the passengers, they use glass for the whole
length. During the summer the doors are removed which admits of
the best ventilation. Altogether they are a very comfortable and
conveniently arranged vehicle, and as a consequence they are used
by the upper ranks of society and by ladies unaccompanied by male
attendants—a practice quite unknown in London'.

In London itself, the various lines were getting known by popular
names. The travellers knew that a *Favourite* went to Islington, or an
*Eagle* to Pimlico. They were also painted different colours, with
the *Eagles* coloured green—that is, until after Queen Victoria had

*A coach being carried on the London and Birmingham Railway, an early example of Motor-rail*

acknowledged the skill of a driver of one in avoiding an accident with Her Majesty's vehicle, after which they were painted blue and the name *Eagle* replaced by the more familiar *Royal Blue.*

Unfortunately the original politeness of the conductors, of which Shillibeer was so proud, gave way to a reputation for rudeness to passengers. They banged the doors, chatted to the driver when they should be attending to the travellers and were generally unhelpful. One complaint concerned an old lady who on entering the door had it shut immediately behind her and the omnibus started before she found a seat. She was suddenly pitched forward into a dark corner, falling against some men who swore violently. She looked more closely at them, and realised they were three convicts chained together on their way to be imprisoned in the Hulks. Screaming she opened the door, only to fall heavily into the road. At this the nimble conductor demanded and obtained her fare, then shouted 'Right—away Bill' and away the omnibus went, leaving her helpless and trembling, sat in the middle of the road.

Another typical trick is recounted in Dickens' *Sketches by Boz*, where a conductor boasts that he can 'chuck an old genlm'n into the bus, shut him in, and rattle off, afore he knows where its agoing to!' Although most complaints were levelled against the conductors, the regular commuters felt that some of the travellers could use some advice, so in *The Times* of January 1836 a list of suggestions was printed which included:

### Omnibus Law

1. Keep your feet off the seats.
2. Do not get into a snug corner yourself and then open the windows to admit a north-wester upon the neck of your neighbour.
3. Have your money ready when you desire to alight.
4. Sit with your limbs straight, and do not let your legs describe an angle of forty-five, thereby occupying the room of two persons.
5. Do not spit on the straw, you are not in a pig-sty but in an omnibus.
6. Behave respectfully to females, and put not an unprotected lass to the blush, because she cannot escape from your brutality.
7. Reserve bickerings and disputes for the open field, the sound of your own voice may be music to your own ears—not so, perhaps, to those of your companion.
8. Refrain from affectation and conceited airs. Remember you are

*Model of a charabanc c.1890. (Science Museum)*

riding a distance for sixpence, which if you made in a hackney coach, would cost you many shillings.

The passengers' intellectual needs were also catered for. Shillibeer supplied newspapers and magazines, but a Mr Cloud whose omnibuses ran from the *White Horse*, Haymarket, had a bookcase in each vehicle, stocked with books by well-known authors. Unfortunately many a passenger, having only reached the third or fourth chapter by the time he reached his destination, found it necessary to remove the book also, and Mr Cloud's bookcases were soon empty! In 1851 a similar experiment with newspapers was tried on the *Favourite* with a notice asking the passengers not only to replace the newspapers on the rack, but also to put a penny in the box towards their cost. Before long the newspapers were gone, and the money boxes rattled with the sound of buttons and metal washers.

The Great Exhibition of 1851 and the remarkable influx of visitors from the country and from abroad brought more and more omnibuses on to the streets. The same year also saw the arrival of Thomas Tilling's first omnibus. This was called *The Times*, and it ran from Peckham to Oxford Circus. One change in his method, was the practice of the omnibus to commence from a given point where the passengers mounted, rather than the usual practice of driving around to fill the coach before setting forth. Also attributed to this period was the knife-board omnibus, in which the roof passengers sat on a long bench running along the centre of the length of the roof. These were introduced by the Economic Conveyance Co. in 1847, but were not fully in use until 1850 when it was usual for these omnibuses to carry twenty-two passengers with nine of them on the roof.

Originally the roof passengers reached their seats by climbing up a ladder. This was later improved in 1853 by the addition of an iron spiral staircase, and in time the seats were fitted across the bus facing forward. An incident involving the upstairs passengers took place in Romford, where the picking-up point in South Street just preceded a low railway bridge. The writer of the article, E. Essam notes 'the wife went upstairs first and found a seat, I was a few seconds behind her as I reached the top. Suddenly a young woman tugged at the tail of my coat, pulling me on to her lap. Only just in time to save me from having my brains knocked out on the top of the arch. It was a shock, and for a moment I sat on the girl's lap, dazed. Then I was filled with gratitude that I kissed the girl for saving my life. But when

*Cruikshank cartoon of the exploding steam coach,* The Rocket. (*Victoria & Albert Museum*)

I got home, the wife so raged at me for allowing the girl to kiss me, that I began to think it would have been better if my brains had been knocked out instead.'

The horsebus remained on the roads until the First World War, but the earlier vehicles on the main coaching routes began to feel the effect of the railways, and from the mid-19th century the tramway came into use. It had been pioneered in 1830 by Abraham Bower, in New York, and after several attempts elsewhere, a line from Marble Arch along the Bayswater Road to Porchester Terrace in London was opened in March 1861. Street tramcars became popular in the late 19th century, and beside the horse-drawn trams, both steam and cable traction were used.

The advent of steam influenced transport in two ways. Walter Hancock invented the steam omnibuses called the *Autopsy* and the *Era* and these were placed on the London roads in 1833. The *Era* which was the better of the two, ran from Paddington to the Bank at a rate of ten miles an hour. It proved a strong rival to the horse-drawn omnibuses, and the proprietors of these complained bitterly about the way in which these steam omnibuses cut up the roads. To stop this, the practice of strewing loose stones on the road was often carried out, in the hope that the stones would disable the steam vehicles. In Gloucester the local authorities were so disturbed about the damage caused by the steam vehicle running between Cheltenham and Gloucester, that they piled loose stones in places to a height of nearly two feet in order to stop its progress. In London Hancock's *Automaton* an improved version with twenty-two seats, continued to run until 1840.

The strongest competition to the coaches was from the new railways, which began to take their toll in the 1830s and 1840s. An advertisement by the Exeter coach proprietor, George H. Small of 1844 explains, 'The opening of the railroad has driven three coaches off the road and depressed all the villages along the line of the road of a certain, cheap and serviceable means of communication with Exeter and Tiverton.'

The Post Office, among others, put coaches on the trains, thus taking even more custom from the road. John Copeland reports on the fire of April 1840 on the Bristol Mail Coach while travelling on the G.W.R. line from London. 'The guards exerted themselves in every possible way by blowing their horns and calling out to the conductor to stop the train, but they could not succeed in making him hear, and

# POLICE NOTICE.

## STREET CROSSING SIGNALS.
### BRIDGE STREET, NEW PALACE YARD.

| CAUTION. | STOP. |
|---|---|

The Semaphore Arms lowered, and by Night with a Green Light.

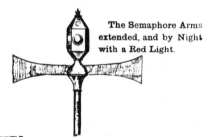
The Semaphore Arms extended, and by Night with a Red Light.

By the Signal "**CAUTION,**" all persons in charge of Vehicles and Horses are warned to pass over the Crossing with care, and due regard to the safety of Foot Passengers.

The Signal "**STOP,**" will only be displayed when it is necessary that Vehicles and Horses shall be actually stopped on each side of the Crossing, to allow the passage of Persons on Foot; notice being thus given to all persons in charge of Vehicles and Horses to stop clear of the Crossing.

## RICHARD MAYNE,

*Commissioner of Police of the Metropolis.*

*The first traffic lights, 1868*

the consequence was that when they arrived at Twyford, the whole front boot was on fire, and of the contents everything was consumed.' Even the railway staff had difficulty at times in remembering they were not on a coach. In 1843 the death of Ralph Walker, a guard, was reported in the *Essex Standard*, 'Having been knocked off the coach on which he was riding, in passing under the bridge at that place, and been crushed to death and frightfully mutilated by the train which followed'.

Although more and more passengers were being carried by rail, there were still plenty of coaches, carriages and cabs on the streets

*A horse bus of the knife-board type common in the 1870s*

to cause confusion. The railway often increased the traffic problem, as the rail passengers going to and from the stations in great numbers needed more vehicles at peak times to take them. A Select Committee was set up in 1855 to consider the traffic crisis and the various witnesses suggested raised footpaths, lowered railways and new roads. They also heard witnesses advocating the abolishment of the turnpikes and the creation of an underground rail link between the main stations. Acts of William III had ordered justices to erect sign posts at crossroads, and as a step further, the Police Notice of 1868 indicates the street crossing signal, which brings us further into the age of modern traffic signals.

Whatever the century or the change in styles of transport, the horse-drawn vehicle survived as a showpiece on State occasions. The original coaches were created for the crowned heads of Europe, and probably the most familiar is the Golden Coronation Coach of Britain. This was designed for George III by Sir William Chambers in 1761. Horace Walpole, writing to Horace Mann notes, 'There is come forth a new State Coach which has cost £8,000. It is a beautiful object,

*London fire engines.* (*Science Museum*)

though crowded with improprieties. Its supports are Tritons ... The crowd to see it on the opening of Parliament was greater than at the Coronation, and much more damage was done!' A contemporary account of the coach describes the ideas behind its design. 'The four angular trees are loaded with trophies, allusive to the victories obtained by Britain during the course of the present glorious war ... on the front panel is represented Britannia seated on a throne, holding in her hand a staff of liberty, attended by Religion, Justice, Wisdom, Valour, Fortitude and Victory presenting her with a garland of laurels.' The inside is lined with crimson velvet richly embroidered with gold. The harness is also of crimson velvet trimmed with buckles of silver gilt. The saddle cloths were of blue velvet embroidered and fringed with gold.

Another splendid vehicle was the Lord Mayor's Coach which was built in 1757 at a cost of over a thousand pounds. It did not originally belong to the London Corporation, as it was built by subscription among the Aldermen. But in 1778 the Corporation bought the coach, had it repaired and the panels repainted. In addition to these 18th century elaborate carriages, the more sober Victorias and barouches are still used on ceremonial occasions, and in their progress down the Mall and into Parliament Square, we catch a glimpse of the elegance of mid-19th century travel.

Some of the coaches carried on for many years, serving the more rural areas. My father who is eighty-three, still recalls the Bath Coach leaving the Bell Inn in Old Town, Swindon, right up into the present century. This was a coach and four run by Hooper Deacon, travelling with a groom, and passengers on the top. Just as the horse-buses were in common use up to the First World War, so the horse-drawn fire-engines, hearses and ambulances were on the town streets during the first quarter of the 20th century. As the motor car and motor bus replaced the coach and omnibus, we find that the early cars were unable to divorce themselves in their design from the original concept of the coach. Emile Levassor, writing in 1893 states, 'We always try and use ordinary methods of construction, and give our carriages a normal appearance.' So we find the motorised Landau, the phaeton with its hood, the Spider exhibiting its rakish elegant lines, even the cab and the Victoria appear with their familiar shapes as horseless carriages. Levassor also commented 'Our problem will not be making them run, but making them sell!' It was unthinkable for *la noblesse* to soil its hands with machinery, and really all that happened was that the engine had taken the place of the horse.

This theme is taken up in the trenchant remarks of *The Times* in 1839. 'Steam, James Watt and George Stephenson have a great deal to answer for. They will ruin the breed of horses, as they have already ruined the innkeepers and the coachmen, many of whom have already been obliged to seek relief at the poor house, or have died in penury and want.'

This, in fact, turned out to be true, for the sound of the engine tolled the death knell of the coaching era.

# MUSEUMS CONTAINING COACH AND CARRIAGE EXHIBITS

BELFAST—Transport Museum, Witham Street, Belfast 4.
Collection contains horse trams, coaches, carriages and vans. Summer: weekdays 11.00–7.00 (Tue. and Wed. 11.00–9.00) Sun. 2.00–7.00; Winter: weekdays 11.00–5.00, Sun. 2.00–5.00. Telephone: Belfast 51519.

CLAPHAM—Museum of British Transport, High Street, Clapham.
This museum contains a representative collection of road vehicles which provided services to the railways. The range includes horse ambulances, horse buses, with the knife-board seat type as well as a replica of George Shillibeer's first omnibus.

CRICK—The Transport Museum, Matlock, Crick.
Unique collection of horse, steam and electrical tramcars and associated equipment. Sat., Sun., Bank Holidays—October 11.00–7.30 or dusk. Tuesday, Wednesdays, Thursdays in June, July and August 10.00–5.00.

DODINGTON CARRIAGE MUSEUM, Chipping Sodbury, Glos.
A museum which concentrates on the horse-drawn vehicle, with actual coaches, prints, coachbuilders' drawings, photographs and models. Carries the visitor through the history of horse transport.

EDINBURGH—Transport Museum, Leith Walk, Edinburgh.
The collection comprises a single gallery with four full size vehicles and other smaller exhibits including photographs, tickets, fare-tables rule books etc.

GLASGOW—Museum of Transport, 25 Albert Drive, G41.
Although concerned chiefly with trams, horse-drawn vehicles are included. A stationbug, the horse charabanc *Ardishaig Belle*, a wagonette, a gig, a brougham and a fine family travelling coach built in 1817.

HULL—Transport Museum, 36 High Street.
The museum contains a collection of thirty large vehicles and twenty smaller ones. The oldest is a barouche of the early 19th century, other exhibits include a cabriolet, post-chaise and two stagecoaches. Among the public transport vehicles is a stagecoach, a hansom cab and the other cases contain harnesses and trappings.

KIRKCALDY—Industrial and Social History Museum. Forth House Kirkcaldy, Fife.

Collection of horse-drawn transport. May to September, Monday to Saturday, 2.00–5.00.

LEICESTER—Museum of Technology, Abbey Pumping Station, Corporation Road, Leicester.

Road transport gallery contains horse-drawn vehicles, cycles, motorcycles and motor cars. Weekdays 10.00–5.30, Sundays 2.00–5.30.

LIVERPOOL—City of Liverpool Museum, William Brown Street.

The basement gallery is devoted to the land transport of the Liverpool region, including horsedrawn and steam road vehicles. Weekdays 10.00–5.00; Sundays 2.00–5.00.

LONDON—Royal Mews, Buckingham Palace Road, S.W.1.

Royal horses and equipages. Wed. and Thurs. 2.00–4.00 (Not Ascot week).

LONDON—Science Museum, Exhibition Road, South Kensington.

A large collection of originals and models of horse-drawn carriages, including a mail-coach of 1827 and the superb Earl of Caledon's Dress Chariot. The earliest vehicle dates from 1700 and progresses through town carriage and broughams to early motor vehicles. Weekdays 10.00–6.00; Sundays 2.30–6.00.

LONDON—Syon Park—The London Transport Museum, Brentford.

A collection of historic vehicles, buses, trams, posters, signs, tickets etc. Included are the Shillibeer Omnibus, a knifeboard Omnibus and the Garden seat Omnibus. Summer: Apr.–Sept. 10.00–7.00; Winter: October–Mar. 10.00–5.00 or dusk.

MAIDSTONE—The Tyrwhitt-Drake Museum of Carriages, Archbishop's Stables, Mill Street.

Horse-drawn vehicles, including most types of State, Official and private carriages. Weekdays 10.00–1.00; 2.00–5.00.

STAFFORDSHIRE County Museum and Mansion House, Nr. Stafford.

Horse-drawn vehicles, farm equipment. Weekdays (except Mondays) 11.00–5.30; Sundays 2.00–5.30. (Closed Oct.–Mar.)

WEST YORKSHIRE Folk Museum, Shibden Hall, Nr. Halifax.

In the stable yards are several coaches, and a very well preserved Shillibeer hearse. Of great interest are the craft workshops, particularly those of the saddle and harness maker, the blacksmith, the farrier and the wheelwright. Apr.–Sept.: weekdays 11.00–7.00, Sun. 2.00–5.00; Oct. and Mar. 11.00–5.00, Sun. 2.00–5.00. (Nov.–Jan. Closed).

# BIBLIOGRAPHY

Adams, W. Bridges. *English pleasure carriages.* Adams & Dart 1837, reprinted 1971.

Anderson, R. C. *and* J. M. *Quicksilver.* David and Charles 1973.

Ashford, L. J. *The history of the Borough of High Wycombe from its origins to 1888.* Routledge & Kegan 1960.

Baines, F. E. *On the track of the mail coaches.* 1895.

Barker, T. C. *and* Robbins, Michael. *A history of London Transport.* 2 vols. Allen & Unwin 1963.

Bartlett, John. *A guide to the transport museum, Kingston upon Hull.* 1971.

Beckmann, Johann. *History of inventions and discoveries.* 1797.

Bodley, Hugh. *Roads.* 1971.

Boswell, James. *The life of Samuel Johnson.* 1971.

Braunder, Michael. *The Georgian gentleman.* Saxon House 1973.

Brown, A. F. J. *Essex at work 1700–1815.* Essex Record Office 1969.

Brown, A. F. J. *English history from Essex Sources 1750–1900.* Essex Record Office 1952.

Burke, Thomas. *The English inn.* Jenkins 1930.

Byng, John. *The Torrington diaries.* Eyre & Spottiswoode 1954.

Chamberlayne, Edward. *Magne Britannia notitia.* 1719.

*Coaching days of England*, with historical commentary by Anthony Burgess. Elek 1966.

Copeland, John. *Roads and their traffic 1750–1850.* David & Charles 1968.

Copeland, John. 'When travellers drove in style'. *Country Life*, 18th April 1963, pp. 834–6.

Croal, Thomas A. *A book about travelling past and present.* W. P. Nimmo 1877.

Cruikshank, R. J. *Charles Dickens and early Victorian England.* Pitman 1949.

*Dictionary of National Biography.*

Edwards, A. C. *English history from Essex Sources 1550–1750.* Essex Record Office 1952.

Essam, E. *Those were the days.* (*Ms* in possession of I. G. Sparkes).

Evelyn *Sir* John. *Diary,* edited by Wm. Bray. n.d.

Fiennes, Celia. *The journeys of Celia Fiennes,* edited by Christopher Morris. Cresset Press 1947.

Fordham, *Sir* George. *The roads of England and Wales and the turnpike system.* Reprinted from *The History Teachers' Miscellany,* vol. V, Nos 5 and 6 (June and July 1927).

Gardiner, Leslie. *Stage coach to John o' Groats.* Hollis & Carter 1961.

Gilbey, *Sir* W. *Early carriages and roads.* 1903

Glasgow Museum of Transport. *Horse-drawn carriages.* 1968.

Harper, Charles G. *Stagecoach and mail in the days of yore.* 2 vols. Chapman & Hall 1903.

Hibbert, Christopher. *Highwaymen.* Weidenfeld & Nicolson 1967.

Hibbs, John. *The history of the British Bus Service.* David & Charles 1968.

Hindley, Geoffrey. *A history of roads.* 1971.

Hunt, J. H. Leigh. *Coaches and coaching.* 1908.

Jackman, W. T. *The development of transportation in modern England.* F. Cass 1962.

Jervis, John. *Horse and carriage oracle.* 1828.

Kandaouroff, *Prince* Dimitry. *Postmarks, cards and covers: collecting postal history.* Peter Lowe 1973.

Lausanne, Edita. *Horseless carriages.* 1968.

Lewins, William. *Her Majesty's mails.* 1864.

A Lover of his country. Pamphlet. 1673.

Macdonald, John. *Travels in various parts.* 1790. Reprinted G. Routledge 1927.

Mackrell, Douglas C. 'A folk museum in the West Riding'. *Country Life,* 6th May 1965. pp. 1099–110.

Moore, Henry Charles. *Omnibuses and cabs: their origin and history.* Chapman & Hall 1902.

Moritz, Carl Philipp. *Travels . . . in England in 1782.* H. Milford 1924.

Moryson, Fynes. *An itinerary written by Fynes Moryson, Gent.* 1617.

Noakes, Aubrey. 'The Christmas legacy of James Pollard.' *Antique Collector,* December 1973.

Parkes, Joan. *Travel in England in the Seventeenth Century.* O.U.P. 1925.

Pepys, Samuel. *Diary.*

Reynardson, C. T. S. Birch. *Down the road.* 1875

Screven, Thomas. *Notebooks* (quoted in Strauss).

Simmons, Jack. *Transport museums in Britain and Western Europe.* Allen & Unwin 1970.

Southey, Robert. *Letters from England.* 1807.

Strauss, Ralph. *Carriages and coaches; their history and their evolution.* Martin Secker 1912.

Sumner, Philip. *Carriages to the end of the nineteenth century.* Science Museum 1970.

Taylor, John. *The world runnes on Wheeles: or oddes betwixt carts and coaches.* 1623.

Thoresby, Ralph. *The diary 1677–1724,* edited by Rev. Joseph Hunter. 1830.

Torqueville, Alexis de. *Journeys to England and Ireland.* Faber 1963.

Tristam W. Outram. *Coaching days and coaching ways.* 1893. Reprinted by E.P. Publishing Ltd 1973.

Unstead, R. J. *Travel by road.* A. & C. Black 1969.

Vale, Edmund. *The mail coachmen of the late eighteenth century.* David & Charles.

Webb, S. & B. *The story of the King's highway.* 1913.

Williams, Montague. Q.C. *Leaves of a life.* Macmillan 1890.

Wingate, John. *Dodington Carriage Museum.* Macmillan Press 1973.

Young, Arthur. *A six weeks tour through the Southern Counties of England and Wales.* 1769.

# INDEX